The
Marriage Enrichment
Handbook

Godly Principles
For
A Successful Marriage

by
Andrew Merritt

Unless otherwise indicated, all Scripture
quotations are taken from the King James
Version of the Holy Bible.

Dedication

In the love of God
this book is dedicated
to hurting marriages everywhere
that through the work of the Holy Spirit
in ministering grace
they may be healed and become
the godly marriages
God ordained them to be.

Foreword

There is hardly an individual who is not aware of the story of the young princess named Cinderella. How intriguing it is that Cinderella's fairy godmother turns the pumpkin into a coach, mice into horses, and the homely into the stunning. However, none of this happens without a warning. Cinderella must leave the ball at midnight; for then reality is to come home.

Midnight. How does one maintain the ideal in face of the real? How does one prevent that coach from becoming a pumpkin, or those beautifully arrayed horses, mice? How does Cinderella maintain her beauty in the face of the darkness? How does one keep the prince around when everything is beginning to turn? A fairy tale? No!

There is no area of life where these questions become more real than in marriage. As Bishop Meritt expresses so forcefully, all too often, the "ideal" becomes an "ordeal," calling for a "new deal."

Are there real answers to the problems that perplex? Are there practical ways that the nightmares of marital life can be resolved so that dreams might be fulfilled? Is there really a "prince" out there for the many "Cinderellas" who are at home--hoping, waiting, wanting, wishing? How are they found? What does one do to attract them? What is the secret in keeping them once discovered?

There is no better book that addresses these issues in a practical way, than that which you are about to read. So, sit back and enjoy, for light is about to penetrate the darkness and bring en[light]enment to your mind, and marriage. And for the single? There is hope for your future.

Pastor Luther Blackwell
Mega Church
Cleveland, Ohio

Table of Contents

Introduction

Accepting Jesus as Lord and Savior is the most important decision you will ever make; choosing a companion in marriage is the second. Deciding who you intend to spend your life with is not a decision to weigh lightly.

It should not be predicated upon how someone looks or based upon what material things they have to offer. A lot of men have made bad decisions based on physical measurements and what they perceived as beauty. Likewise, many women have made the wrong decision over dinner, allowing their emotions to lead them. Choosing a companion must be a decision that is made very carefully. It is not a physical or emotional experience--it's a spiritual matter.

The average person who gets married is not prepared for marriage. If some people today had known Jesus and lived according to the Word of God before they married, they would not have married their current spouse. However, God honors marriage because He is the Institutor of it. Every time there is a marriage performed between believers, these three are always present--the bride, the groom, and God.

According to God's Word, every bad marriage can become good. You just need to find the principles He has established in His Word and implement them into your life. You may say, ''Well, some negative things have happened; we have experienced some hurts, bitterness, and strife.'' But God can touch your life and make it seem as if those things never happened, regardless of what your spouse has done.

In Philippians 3:13, the Apostle Paul admonishes us by saying, "...forgetting those things which are behind...." It is only in this "forgetting" that we can make the marital progress that God has designed for us, and find the marriage enrichment that He has ordained for us.

It is my prayer that as you read this book, God will unfold before you and put deep within you His truths concerning the marital union. God bless you.

Pastor Andrew Merritt
Straight Gate Church

Acknowledgements

Special thanks to
Karen V. Brown
for her editorial assistance.

Also, to my publishers,
Timothy and Tanya Stokes,
who have toiled and labored with me, countless hours.
Through all of the last minute changes and troubles,
they stuck right with me to the bitter end.

Chapter One

Five Bonds of Marriage

Webster's Dictionary defines marriage as ''the state of being married; relation between husband and wife; married life; wedlock; matrimony; the act of marrying; wedding; any close union.'' To enrich means ''to make rich or richer; to give more wealth; to give greater value, importance, effectiveness; to decorate; adorn; to fertilize; to add vitamins, minerals to.'' Marriage is more than two people getting a license, going to a preacher or judge, and living together. Marriage is a total, lifetime commitment; it is a bonding together. Let's look at the five bonds that constitute marriage.

MARRIAGE IS A LEGAL BOND:

The state of Michigan is responsible for granting the right of marriage. In the state of Michigan, a man must be 21 years of age to be married without parental approval; a woman must be 18 years of age. If she is only 16 years old and he's 18, a court order must be obtained and their parents must appear before the judge. If the couple's ages are 13 and 14, they must get a decree from the court.

A marriage is legalized when the marriage certificate is returned to the state.

A record is kept of every marriage performed at the Straight Gate Church. Everyone who comes to us must provide a birth certificate for age verification. It doesn't matter if you look your age or not--marriage is a legal bond and proof is required.

MARRIAGE IS A COVENANT BOND:

The word covenant means ''agreement.'' When a couple gets married, they enter into an agreement or a covenant bond. They make vows to one another before God and man, and they are expected to uphold them. Marriage is a binding agreement--it places the man and woman under a legal obligation.

MARRIAGE IS A SEXUAL BOND:

Once the legal union has been established through the exchange of vows before God and man, you can enter into the sexual part of the relationship. There is, however, something very important that most people overlook: marriage is not solely physical--it is also spiritual.

The problem with most people, particularly those still in the world, is that they have entered marriage strictly from a physical perspective. Most Christians, although born-again, have not yet deprogrammed themselves to the things of the world. Consequently, they have not yet reprogrammed themselves with the will and Word of God. This means they do not know right from wrong. These are Spirit-filled people with worldly concepts about marriage. God designed and created marriage. He set the terms for marriage.

MARRIAGE IS AN ECONOMICAL BOND:

I always advise young women by saying, "Do not marry a man who is not going to take care of you." Marriage is an economical responsibility. God placed the burden for the care of the wife and the family upon the man. This is a great responsibility for the man and he should not enter into it lightly. The woman's well-being is in his hands; God has charged him with her care. Breaking this bond violates the marriage covenant and it is a sin against God.

MARRIAGE IS A SOCIAL BOND:

Regardless of how many people get married and divorced, our society still recognizes marriage. Because God ordained it, it is still looked upon as that standard of relationships. Although it is being challenged from every walk of life, it is still God's prescribed way.

Marriage can also be described as God's relationship with His church. The reason many saints do not understand the natural marital union is because they have never received the revelation of marriage in the spiritual arena. Marriage is more than just a natural union--it is spiritual. Revelation 19:6-9 says:

> *And I heard as it were the voice of a great multitude and as the voice of many waters, and as the voice of mighty thunderings, saying, "Alleluia: for the Lord God omnipotent reigneth.*
>
> *Let us be glad and rejoice and give honor to him for the marriage of the Lamb is come, and his wife: [the Church] hath made herself ready.*

And to her was granted that she should be arrayed in fine linen, clean and white: for the fine linen is the righteousness of saints."

And He saith unto me, "Write, Blessed are they which are called unto the marriage supper of the Lamb." And He said unto me, "These are the true sayings of God."

The whole terminology of marriage is couched in the Jewish culture. If a man or woman cohabited with someone other than their covenant party, they were killed. The Church has committed spiritual adultery, because it only understands marriage from the context of the world. Marriage is not a trial, where you test it out to see if it will work. Marriage is a commandment from God; it is a responsibility and a commitment.

If under the Jewish covenant the adulterer forfeited his life, what position are we placed in when we say that we love Jesus, but really love the world, thereby committing spiritual adultery?

A Wise Builder

Therefore whosoever heareth these sayings of mine, and doeth them, I will liken him unto a wise man, which built his house upon a rock:

And the rain descended, and the floods came, and the winds blew, and beat upon that house; and it fell not: for it was founded upon a rock.

*And every one that heareth these sayings of mine,
and doeth them not shall be likened unto a foolish
man, which built his house upon the sand:*

*And the rain descended, and the floods came, and
the winds blew, and beat upon that house; and it
fell: and great was the fall of it.*

Matthew 7:24-27

To capture the Greek connotation of this Scripture, read it again, substituting the word "family" for the word "house." The Rock is Jesus, or the Word of God. Your family must be built upon the Word of God to withstand the storms of life. Yet even when you build upon the Word of God, these storms will still come. The difference is that the family who has the Word as its foundation will stand--no matter what hell throws against it!

On the other hand, if you do not build your house on the Word of God, when the storms of life come, as they inevitably will, your family will suffer. Jesus said, "...and it fell: and great was the fall of it." God holds us accountable for the truth that we receive; we are expected to walk according to it. James 4:17 says, "Therefore to him that knoweth to do good, and doeth it not, to him it is sin."

Now most people believe that in this Scripture Jesus is referring to both the saved and the unsaved, but He's not; Jesus is speaking only to the people of God. He's saying that when you hear a sermon or read a book, the Holy Spirit is present to witness to the truths proclaimed. Therefore, when you hear the Word of God and do it, God compares you to a wise man.

You may never have been wise before, but obey the Word of God, and you become wise. The Bible doesn't say that you're wise before you apply the Word. It says that when you become a doer of the Word wisdom is attributed to you, because the Word of God is filled with wisdom. When you hear and do, you're like a wise man. But when you don't apply what you hear, you're like a foolish man. It's not that you're a fool, but God compares you to a foolish man because foolish people don't really hear the Word.

When you embrace the Word of God to obey it, you're building with God's wisdom. A house (family) built on the Word cannot be penetrated by the devil, because it is God who is actually doing the building through you. And it's building on the Word that is the key.

I've seen people shout, dance, speak in tongues, and fall out on the floor in response to a good sermon, but that's not building on the Word of God. When it comes to putting the Word of God into operation, they fail miserably. People can have the best marriage this side of heaven if they make the quality decision to obey God's commands: ''Through wisdom is an house [family] builded; and by understanding it is established: and by knowledge shall the chambers be filled with all precious and pleasant riches.'' (Proverbs 24:3-4)

There are two classes of people in the earth: the wise and the foolish. The wise man hears the revelation of the Word of God and responds favorably--he builds his house (family) according to God's plan. The foolish man hears the same Word, but he denies what he hears. He doesn't respond favorably--he cannot be persuaded to act upon what he has heard. Yet he continues to build.

Whether you know it or not, you are building your life now. You have to learn what tools you must use in order to build properly. When Jesus spoke the parable of building on a rock or on sand, He was really saying that if you build with foolishness (materials that are not of God) you are going to fail. But He also made it clear that everyone has the opportunity to build upon a good foundation, through Jesus Christ. This foundational element is key in the formation of a good marriage.

Note that Jesus said the storms of life come to every house. The winds of opposition beat and blow on every house. But when a house is built on the Rock, which is Jesus, He will protect that family through every storm. This is not so with the house that is built upon sand (the world's standards).

I'm reminded of an incident that happened when I was vacationing with my wife. We were strolling along the beach in Acapulco. She finally coaxed me to walk in the water. As we walked, we paused to watch the big waves as they drifted upon the shore. Right where I had been standing, the sand would disappear as the wave returned to the sea. This is what happens when you build according to the world's standards. Failure may not occur today or tomorrow, but it's coming. It may be 20 years down the road, but failure is inevitable when you build upon sand.

Built By God

> *Except the Lord build the house [or the family], they labor in vain that build it: except the Lord keep the city, [or the family], the watchmen waketh but in vain. It is vain for you to rise up early, to sit up late, to eat the bread of sorrows: for so he giveth his beloved sleep.*
>
> Psalms 127:1-2

Are you resting well at night? You should be, because God has promised it to you. To gain insight into this Scripture, look at it through the eyes of Jewish people.

When the Jews built houses, they built them high upon

a hill. They began by building the wall; afterwards, they would erect the house upon the wall. The guard would then look over the wall or march along the wall to see who was coming. If an enemy approached the house, he could be easily seen by the guard from afar. Solomon is saying that while in the natural realm men build and guard their homes, in the spiritual realm the Lord must build and keep the family; otherwise, you are wasting your time.

Many people today, particularly in the church, are consumed with acquiring things. Some seek to acquire an education, while others seek material gain. Their emphasis is in the wrong place. Jesus said, ''But seek ye first the kingdom of God, and his righteousness; and all these things shall be added unto you'' (Matthew 6:33).

Solomon said, if you build a house without God, it is vain (useless, futile, ineffective, unproductive). In essence, he was warning us that the watchman, the one who normally watches for you, is going to fall asleep. Today, many people are in a state of stupor in their marriages. God has called me as a watchman on the wall to awaken you. In the name of Jesus, you must get back on the wall and guard your marriage from the wiles of the enemy.

Hollywood's portrayal of marriage as a fantasy concludes with the couple standing, kissing, and living happily ever after; they will never have a struggle. In reality, however, life is a struggle. When two people make the quality decision to become one, it is just the beginning of the struggle. These two must allow the Lord to build their house, or it will not withstand the pressures of the flood.

Chapter Two

Created in His Image

In the beginning God created the heaven and the earth.

And the earth was without form, and void; and darkness was upon the face of the deep. And the Spirit of God moved upon the face of the waters.

Genesis 1:1-2

The word Genesis means "beginning." Genesis is the book of beginnings. In the book of Genesis, through revelation knowledge, God unfolds the beginning to Moses.

Everything God created was perfect, yet this verse speaks of a chaotic situation. The flood God sent during the time of Noah was not the first flood; it was the second. The books of Isaiah and Jeremiah speak of God's destruction of the then-known world--the earth was covered with water. God destroyed the world because of the rebellion of both Lucifer and the pre-Adamic creation.

Then, in Genesis, God begins to restore the world. He

uses the word ''good'' seven times. Every time God restores something, He calls it good. But He called His creation of man ''very good'' because He created man in His image and after His likeness. The Hebrew word for image is ''the exact duplicate--nothing varying.''

> *And God said, "Let us make man in our image, after our likeness: and let them have dominion over the fish of the sea, and over the fowl of the air, and over the cattle, and over all the earth, and over every creeping thing that creepeth upon the earth."*
>
> *So God created man in his own image, in the image of God created he him; male and female created he them.*
>
> *And God blessed them, and God said unto them, "Be fruitful, and multiply, and replenish the earth, and subdue it: and have dominion over the fish of the sea, and over the fowl of the air, and over every living thing that moveth upon the earth..."*
>
> *And God saw every thing that he had made, and, behold, it was very good. And the evening and the morning were the sixth day.*
>
> Genesis 1:26-28,31

Man is an expression of God. He is the only creature in the universe who can talk face to face with God Almighty. Only man can feel the touch of the living God--mouth to mouth, breast to breast, and heart to heart. This is the type of relationship God desires to have with man. The only way He can get it is to reproduce Himself through men and women who have a revelation of the marriage covenant. Jesus prayed, "...that they may be one, even as we are one: I in them, and thou in me, that they may be made perfect in one..." (John 17:22-23).

And the Psalmist wrote:

> *What is man, that thou art mindful of him? and the son of man, that thou visitest him?*
>
> *For thou hast made him a little lower than the angels, and hast crowned him with glory and honour.*
>
> *Thou madest him to have dominion over the works of thy hands; thou hast put all things under his feet.*

Psalms 8:4-6

According to the Hebrew translation, the word "angels" implies that God made man a little lower than Eliohim. In other words, God could not express Himself in the angelic, animal, or vegetable kingdoms so He expressed Himself in man. Man has been made a little lower than God. God invested Himself, disrobed Himself, revealed Himself, and deposited Himself in man.

Man Needs Companionship

> *And the LORD God took the man, and put him into the garden of Eden to dress it and to keep it.*
>
> *And the LORD God commanded the man, saying,*

"Of every tree of the garden thou mayest freely eat:

But of the tree of the knowledge of good and evil, thou shalt not eat of it: for in the day that thou eatest thereof thou shalt surely die."

And the LORD God said, "It is not good that the man should be alone; I will make him an help meet for him."

Genesis 2:15-18

God restored the earth and made man after His own image and likeness, giving him dominion, kingship, and rulership in the earth. God placed Adam in the garden of Eden to dress and keep it. Then, because there was no help found meet or suitable for the man, God said, "It is not good for the man to be alone."

God created Adam and put him in a perfect environment, yet there was one more thing Adam required. In the inception of human history, God purposefully created Adam with a lack so that when God supplied it, Adam would appreciate that need being fulfilled. God put Adam to sleep and took one of his ribs to create woman, thereby filling the lack. This is how God ordained marriage.

And while the woman was created for the purpose of being a helpmeet to the man, God never intended for her to be under the man's foot.

The Dispensation of Innocence

A dispensation is a period of time in which man's obedience is tested in respect to some specific revelation from

God.

Adam was created innocent--not perfect, just innocent. He was to receive knowledge from God. During this period of innocence, Adam was totally dependent upon God. The Scriptures state that "in the cool of the day" God would come down and converse with Adam (Genesis 3:8).

It's interesting to note that even though God wanted to spend time with Adam, He never interrupted Adam's labor. It's amazing how some people do not want to work; they want to sit around all day and read Scriptures.

But God put Adam in the garden of Eden to work. And work he did! God established the principle of work before the fall; work has always been a Godly principle. Someone once said, "Work is a curse." That's a lie! Work is not a curse; you're cursed if you don't work. If an able-bodied person refuses to work, God doesn't even want that person to eat (2 Thessalonians 3:10).

When God created every animal, He created them male and female together. But when He created man, He created Adam first and then Eve. God took time to create a specific woman for Adam. He created a woman who was precisely what Adam needed. She looked exactly the way Adam wanted her to look; she was the right height and measurements for him. Adam was satisfied with her physically, and she was the perfect spiritual partner. She met his needs emotionally and intellectually.

In the Hebrew language, the word "woman" means "Ishshah." Ishshah talks about a love song. It means she is everything that a man needs. She is his help meet, the woman that he wants and desires.

The Wife as Completer

The creation of woman emanated from God, not Adam.

God decided to make a help meet for Adam.

> *And the LORD God caused a deep sleep to fall upon Adam, and he slept: and he took one of his ribs, and closed up the flesh instead thereof;*
>
> *And the rib, which the LORD God had taken from man, made he a woman, and brought her unto the man.*
>
> *And Adam said, "This is now bone of my bones, and flesh of my flesh: she shall be called Woman, because she was taken out of Man."*

Genesis 2:21-23

God saw that it wasn't good for a man to be alone, so He made a help meet for him. The man is incomplete without the woman. Men, it will help you in your relationship if you realize that your wife is your completer, and treat her accordingly. And wives, you must understand that you are the man's completer, not his competition.

While the wife is the completer of her husband, it does not mean she becomes a duplicate of him. Rather, everything that he is not she becomes, completing and complimenting him. The wife will always be different from her husband, and he must recognize that she has certain qualities, abilities, and sensitivities that he does not possess. She provides what is necessary to make him a complete unit. She can only do this, however, when she is recognized as the completer.

For example, I love to talk; I can talk all night long. I'm quick to answer and give my opinion. My wife, on the other hand, is just the opposite. In our initial stages of marriage, I wondered what I had gotten myself into, because when I asked her a question, she'd take two minutes to answer. I wasn't used to that at all. She was quiet, but I was expecting her to be like me. I remember wondering if something was wrong with her. But I have since discovered that she is a woman of very few words. While it takes me days to get around to what I want to say, she has the ability to express herself very directly, getting right to the point. She always provides helpful input.

Another example of our differences and her ability to compliment and complete, became evident in my wife's approach to meeting our financial obligations. Before we married, my approach to paying bills was that I had a 30 day grace period; and I used every bit of it. My wife's philosophy, however, was to pay the bills a week before they were due. I thought it was crazy to pay them early. But my wife saw it differently.

She was concerned about our integrity and what others thought about her word; I couldn't have cared less. But when she explained to me that she was trying to protect our credit rating and save money on interest payments, I couldn't argue; she was right. After 14 years of marriage, we still do it her way.

It's important to understand that even though I yielded to my wife in the matter of paying our bills, I did not relinquish my authority. I simply came to understand and accept that she was sent to be my help meet. Because she is the woman with whom I am going to experience success in every area of my life, I must do everything necessary to bring out the best in her, to make her feel good about herself, and to make her feel that she is a part of me. I cannot ignore or push her into the background; she is my wife and she belongs by my side. I feel so strongly about our relationship and her place in my life that I will tell anyone, "If you don't like my wife, you don't like me!" This is the type of unity (oneness) that God is calling for in marriage.

Adam was created in the image and likeness of God. Because he possessed the image and likeness of God, Adam had the mind of God. When Adam saw Eve and called her "woman," he was speaking the mind of God. Adam had a perfect revelation about Eve--he knew she was to complete him because she was taken out of him.

A Subtle Deception

> *Now the serpent was more subtle than any beast of the field which the LORD God had made. And he said unto the woman, "Yea, hath God said, 'Ye shall not eat of every tree of the garden?'"*
>
> *And the woman said unto the serpent, "We may eat of the fruit of the trees of the garden:*
>
> *But of the fruit of the tree which is in the midst of the garden, God hath said, 'Ye shall not eat of it, neither shall ye touch it, lest ye die.'"*

Genesis 3:1-3

This passage of Scripture illustrates how the devil attempts to come at people. He doesn't know your thoughts, neither is he omniscient; therefore, he doesn't know everything. He knows you when you open your mouth; when you begin to talk you reveal yourself to the devil. When Eve told the devil of God's command, Satan took that as an open channel through which to operate. When you carelessly speak, you provide a channel for the devil to move in your life. When you make statements like, "If this doesn't work out, I'm going to get a divorce," or "If he doesn't change, I am going to leave him,''you are inviting trouble. Satan will move against you through your words and apply pressure to your situation.

We need to understand that our conduct outside of the church walls will have an impact on our lives. It's not hard for most people to live upright in church; it's returning home that presents most people with the test. It's easy to give the impression that your marriage is together while you're in the midst of others. But what happens when you get home? Is that when the arguing starts and the unpaid bills and the children's behavior become an issue?

We must realize that Satan uses every avenue he can to gain an inroad into our lives. As you live together, and your funny, little ways begin to show, your marriage will be tested. The issue is, what will your response be? Will your response open the door to the devil, or will your response slam the door right in his ugly face? Harmony and trust in marriage will block the devil's advances.

> *But of the tree of the knowledge of good and evil, thou shalt not eat of it: for in the day that thou eatest thereof thou shalt surely die.*

> Genesis 2:17

Note that God said, ''...thou shalt surely die.'' There was no room for doubt in what God spoke: If they ate, they would die. Period. But notice the devil's tactics. He began to pervert what God had said: ''And the serpent said unto the woman, 'Ye shall not surely die: For God doth know that in the day ye eat thereof, then your eyes shall be opened, and ye shall be as gods, knowing good and evil.'''

We are admonished in Revelation 22:18-19 not to add to or take away from the Scriptures. But this doesn't stop the devil. He'll do whatever he has to in order to trip you up--including perverting God's word.

In his conversation with Eve, Satan was implying that God was withholding something from her and Adam. In other words, he was telling Eve, "You can't trust God!" It's the same thing with our marriages--most people don't trust God.

It was never the will of God that man should know evil. When the devil comes to you and says, "Get a divorce," he's really saying, "Know evil." I understand that there are exceptions, such as in the case of fornication. However, no one goes through a separation and divorce, with all of the fighting and hard words that usually accompany it, without getting hurt.

The problem with the Church is that it knows more about evil than good. Preachers talk about evil more than about good, and I'm not necessarily referring to sin, either. When you come out of the world, you already have enough evil thoughts. Your mind has to be deprogrammed and then reprogrammed with good thoughts. This is why many people have misconceptions about God. And this is why so many people do not know how to operate in marriage.

And consider this: God may have to change you in order to change your marriage. So forget about changing your spouse--you change!

A Godly Image

> *And when the woman saw that the tree was good for food, and that it was pleasant to the eyes, and a tree to be desired to make one wise, she took of the fruit thereof, and did eat, and gave also unto her husband with her; and he did eat.*

> *And the eyes of them both were opened, and they*

knew that they were naked; and they sewed fig leaves together, and made themselves aprons.

And they heard the voice of the LORD God walking in the garden in the cool of the day: and Adam and his wife hid themselves from the presence of the LORD God amongst the trees of the garden.

And the LORD God called unto Adam, and said unto him, "Where art thou?"

And he said, "I heard thy voice in the garden, and I was afraid, because I was naked; and I hid myself."

And he said, "Who told thee that thou wast naked? Hast thou eaten of the tree, whereof I commanded thee that thou shouldest not eat?"

And the man said, "The woman whom thou gavest to be with me, she gave me of the tree, and I did eat."

And the LORD God said unto the woman, "What is this that thou hast done?" And the woman said, "The serpent beguiled me, and I did eat."

And the LORD God said unto the serpent, "Because thou hast done this, thou art cursed above all cattle, and above every beast of the field; upon thy belly shalt thou go, and dust shalt thou eat all the days of thy life:

And I will put enmity between thee and the woman, and between thy seed and her seed; it shall bruise thy head, and thou shalt bruise his heel."

Unto the woman he said, "I will greatly multiply thy sorrow and thy conception; in sorrow thou shalt bring forth children; and thy desire shall be to thy husband, and he shall rule over thee."

Genesis 3:6-16

When God created man, He desired to have a people who had His mind, image, and likeness. At the inception of the husband and wife relationship, both the man and the woman were heirs together of the grace of life. The man was to be the leader and provider, and he was responsible for the relationship; the woman was to follow and complete the man. God didn't originally plan for the man to rule the woman. But Eve was deceived by the serpent and partook of the fruit. And when Adam took the fruit with her, he failed to exercise his God-given leadership. They threw away their godly-covering when they turned to sin; this caused their relationship to change.

In spite of this plunge into sin, God has continued to express His love for the entire human family. But most preachers, teachers, and other people who read the Bible make a mistake. They focus on the rulership issue in Genesis 3:16, forgetting that it is a part of the curse. They need to remember that in spite of the curse, God continues to operate in love towards mankind. The focus should be on love, not rulership.

Genesis 3:16 also speaks of the woman's "desire." In the Hebrew language, the word "desire" means to overtake or overcome. Because of sin and disobedience to God's word, Adam and Eve received the Satanic nature--they came under the curse. The woman's natural desire changed--she no longer wanted to be subject to the man. She now wanted to lead or overtake him. And that's the real story behind Genesis 3:16--

the curse changed the focus of the relationship from one of love to one of rulership.

Dual Submission

Most people have never been taught or exposed to godly examples of how a man should treat his wife and how a woman should treat her husband. It's an issue of dual submission.

Women don't need to be delivered by joining the feminist movement. Whether you know it or not, you were liberated nearly 2,000 years ago at Calvary, when Jesus Christ, the Son of the Living God, laid down His life. He liberated women and took them back to a place of prominence, positioning them right next to the man. As a result, your liberation comes to the church in the form of dual submission (Ephesians 5:21). The man is to be the leader; the woman is assigned to pray for him so that he will be a good one. The success, happiness, and prosperity of women is tied to their husbands.

When you, as a wife, leave your position as a completer you will put your marriage in jeopardy. When you, as a husband, permit your wife to be neglected, you will likewise put your marriage in jeopardy.

Adam failed to minister to Eve. If he had met her needs, she never would have listened to the serpent, Satan. That's why we have the dilemmas in our homes, and that's why the devil is wreaking havoc in our nation. He's destroying America by destroying our homes; and if he destroys the homes, he will destroy the church.

Prior to the fall, Adam and Eve walked in unity. As they honored and feared God under the covenant, they prospered. But on the day that Eve, acting on the words of the devil, partook of the forbidden fruit, a separation came between her and Adam.

After the fall, Adam no longer called Eve his compl-eter. He named her after the fall occurred, calling her Eve, which means "life-giver." Adam chose Eve's name because she became the mother of all living, fallen humanity. They never produced the God-kind of creatures that God intended for them to produce, as He stated in Genesis 1:28, "... Be fruitful, and multiply, and replenish the earth ...." Instead, they reproduced after their own kind--fallen humanity: "And Adam called his wife's name Eve [life-giver]; because she was the mother of all living [fallen humanity]" (Genesis 3:20).

"Ye Shall be as Gods"

Genesis 3:5 declares, "...and ye shall be as gods, knowing good and evil." This strong statement implies that Adam did not share what he was receiving from God with Eve. Men are not to go home and park themselves under a television set. The man, as the high priest, is to call his family together and pray to God.

You can have the God-kind of marriage, but you're going to have to make the quality decision to divorce yourself from some preconceived ideas about your role in marriage. Some people will have to humble themselves, while others will have to repent to their spouses for past failures. If you've been wrong, confess it to God; do not try to act as if your misbehavior doesn't exist. Unfortunately, many people are so indoctrinated that they don't want to admit that they are wrong. Instead, they use all types of jargon, like "I missed it" or "I blew it." A husband could transform his marriage immediately if he would just admit to his wife that he's been wrong, and ask for her forgiveness.

An Expression of Love

God could not express Himself as He wanted to through the vegetable, animal, or even the angelic creation; so He made man in His image and after His likeness. Because of His great love for mankind, God instituted marriage as the seedbed of a family that expresses this love.

When God made man, He purposed to express His great love for man through the human family by way of the marriage covenant. This God-ordained method requires a man to leave his mother and father, cleaving to his wife; the two become one, reproducing children to replenish the earth.

Chapter Three

Leaving and Cleaving

Therefore shall a man leave his father and his mother, and shall cleave unto his wife: and they shall be one flesh.

And they were both naked, the man and his wife, and were not ashamed.

Genesis 2:24-25

There are four places in the Scriptures where we find statements concerning the man leaving his parents and cleaving to his wife. The first time is in Genesis, when Adam prophesied upon being presented with the woman. Then in the words of Jesus, as found in the gospels of Matthew and Mark.

And finally the Apostle Paul expresses it in Ephesians.

It was God's idea from the beginning for mankind to have the God-kind of marriage. But then sin entered into the picture, and the curse changed the marital relationship. God, however, did not change His desire and purpose for the marriage union. And through salvation, God has made a way for His method and idea of marriage to become a reality in every couple's life.

God has placed the responsibility of building the family upon the male. God holds the man spiritually accountable for the family. God spoke to man through the mouth of Adam saying, ''...a man [shall] leave his father and mother ....'' Then he is to go, with his wife, and establish another (his own) family.

No individual should ever consider marrying if their potential mate has not matured enough to leave his or her parents. This does not mean leaving a distinct place or locality. The Bible is talking about cutting the strings of parental influence. The man's leaving has to be complete in that he leaves both physically and emotionally.

Yes, the Scripture does say, ''Honor thy father and mother ...'' (Ephesians 6:2). Sons and daughters are to help their parents when they have need, but there still must be a separation.

God is saying that if you are going to establish a family, you must first leave the family you were born into. For the sake of a successful marriage, you must be willing to leave every relationship that you have. No other relationship should supercede marriage. No one should hinder your marriage--not your mother, father, sister, or brother--and nothing should get in the way.

If you are a man who is contemplating matrimony, do not take your bride to live with her in-laws (your family). It would be better for you to stay in a one-room shelter. You must live separately so that you can establish your own family. You will not be able to do this the way God intended if you remain under your parent's influence; that is why separation is necessary.

Many people have never really left home. Some people have physically been away from home for 30 years, yet they cannot go a day without talking to their parents. They can't even make a decision without consulting their parents! Marital conflict is often the result of this dependency. A good relationship with their spouse is jeopardized because of this lingering involvement with the in-laws. In their mind, they've never left home.

Then, there are others who have left home, but something else takes priority and interferes with the marital relationship. It may be business or pleasure, but it gets in the way. Some people don't know when to stop working; others don't seem to realize that "a night out with the boys" can be a problem. If you want to have your night out with the boys (or the girls), why did you get married in the first place? Outside of your relationship with God, nothing is to take precedence over your spouse. You must be willing to leave all and then cleave to your wife.

The strongest Hebrew definition for cleave is "submit." You are to leave your father and your mother and become glued or submitted to your wife. In other words, when people see you, your wife should be by your side. This is the cleaving part. You and your wife should be so close that it is as if you are cemented together. You become one. The two become one flesh. God wants you to never get away from each other.

If you apply the Word of God to your marriage, regardless of the current condition of it, you and your spouse can become glued together as one flesh. You may say, "We are far apart," but the Word is like glue; if you apply it, it will bring you together. It will rectify any situation. The Word of God is energized with life, power, and the very nature of God.

As children, we used to take brown paper bags, blow them up, and pop them. That is what the Word of God does. You take the Word of God, apply it to your failing marriage and let it go. The life in the Word of God blows all that which is wrong out of your marriage.

Jeremiah 1:12 says, "... I will hasten my word to perform it." God promised to bring down the high mountains; He promised to fill the valleys; He promised to make the crooked ways straight and the rough ways smooth. When you obey God, He will keep His promises!

<u>Becoming One</u>

When you leave your mother and father, God intends for you to cleave and become one flesh. This produces an intimate, sexual relationship between a husband and wife.

God established the terms of a marital relationship with these twenty-two words: "Therefore shall a man leave his father and his mother, and shall cleave unto his wife: and they shall be one flesh" (Genesis 2:24).

While she was yet in her youth, I counseled my daughter, Rachelle, concerning marriage. I said to her, "When you reach a certain age, you are going to go to college, get married, and never return to live in this house again." Children must be reared to be responsible adults. At a certain point, children must leave and their parents are no longer responsible for them. They should cleave to their spouses and become one.

The act of becoming one is explosive: It tears at people.

When people initially marry they are not one; they are becoming one. Two personalities are going to be merged, blended, and glued together. They must learn how to think alike and how to be sensitive to each other. They must learn to care for each other and plan together.

The most important ingredient that men tend to leave out of their marital relationship is the cleaving. Another aspect of the definition of cleave is ''to be chased.'' You should never get to the place where you quit chasing your wife. A husband must never become so confident with his wife that he stops pursuing her.

Marriage is a continuous honeymoon. There should be a flower shop representative who knows you by name, and who knows the type of flowers your wife likes. There should be a candy store clerk who, because of your regular visits, knows exactly what your wife prefers. Husbands should know their wife's dress, coat, and shoe size. This is an important aspect of becoming one. This is part of chasing and pursuing.

Have you ever seen rivers flow? They start individually, but at some geographical point they merge, becoming one. Once they become one, there is a combustion, a force, that accompanies their unity, their oneness.

This is the same principle that applies to marriage. Only in the spirit world can one plus one equal one.

When Spirit-filled people become one, they become a force; there is combustion and power. Just as when the individual streams of water connect, and there is an overpowering that causes the river to overflow, so too it is with marriage. When two become one, there is an adjustment period that occurs while the blending takes place; there is some friction and turmoil. But just as when the streams continue to flow, eventually smoothing out and becoming one river, so too it is with the marital union--if you continue, you will become one.

All of your life, you've been an individual. Then all of a sudden, you contemplate marriage. This is when you must understand that the God-kind of marriage has no place for individualism. A common phrase in today's society is "trial marriage." There is no such thing! Do not allow the devil to deceive you. Marriage is a command from the Lord. It is not something to be done on a trial basis.

Hollywood's Example

The world says, "Live together for a while to see if you like it." God is against this type of union. God only condones the marital union which He initiated. Don't let talk show hosts or movie stars determine how you think about marriage.

Hollywood is a fantasy world. It blinds people's eyes so they cannot see to believe the truth that is found in God's Word. Why would you want to listen to people who have been married and divorced over and over again? They can't counsel you on how to have a successful marriage: their lifestyle is not your example! For the Bible says in Hebrews 13:4, "...whoremongers and adulterers God will judge." Godly counsel is the only counsel that will promote a godly marriage.

The Little Things

... [it's] the little foxes, that spoil the vines....

Song of Solomon 2:15

When Israel built their houses, they first erected walls around them. Vines would grow over the walls and the little foxes would come and dig the vines up. This destroyed the roots, and the vines eventually died.

It's no different in our lives and our marriages. When you violate the Word of God, you put death into operation regarding your situation. It's the little things which you think are not important that can destroy a marriage.

Whether we know it or not, we are all a product of our parent's influence. If you came out of a home in which your father and mother did not express the God-kind of love, you have been influenced by that type of marriage. That influence shows up in the little things you do. So God commands you to leave that former influence in order that He might show you how to establish the God-kind of marriage.

A Godly Viewpoint

Look at your marriage through the eyes of God. I will use my marriage as an example. We are madly in love with each other. Yet when I look at God's plan for marriage, what He has designed, I can see that we have not even touched the utopia or zenith of that one relationship which is a type of the relationship that Christ has for His church.

There are many people whose marriages need an overhaul; you need a word from God. Because the Word of God is powerful, energized with the very life and nature of God, it has the ability to renew your marriage. You need to put God's word into operation in your marriage--it will change things! The way you do this is to allow the Word to change you. Through the witness of your transformation, your spouse will be changed.

Since God has ordained marriage, we need to hear and understand what God's mind is concerning marriage. You can go to any secular bookstore and find books on marriage, but that's not what you need. You need God's viewpoint.

Lee Iacocca was featured in a TV commercial where he said, "If you can find a better automobile than a Chrysler, buy it." And I'm saying this to you: You will never find a better manual on marriage than the Word of God. It is the blueprint for marriage and every other area of your life. You need to open it and find out what God has to say.

The problem is, many people don't read their Bibles. Consequently, they have no idea what God's plan for their life is. They're not living life to it's fullness. They go to church just to be in attendance; there's no life in it. But if you really want to enjoy life, if you really want to understand God's plan and purpose for man in the earth, find out what the Lord is saying.

If married people in the church would follow God's outline for marriage, the unsaved would be lining up along the church walls to hear the gospel. Couples would seek you out for marriage counseling because you would be producing the fruit of a Godly marriage--you would have the answers to their problems. Two Spirit-filled believers becoming one are a powerful tool as they witness to God's ideal for marriage.

We are a long way from the oneness that God has designed for us. Yet the revelation I've received on relationships has caused me to establish a high goal in that area. The first step toward that goal is applying the Word of God to our lives. Hebrews 11:3 says, "Through faith we understand that the worlds were framed by the word of God, so that things which are seen were not made of things which do appear." The Word can take your marriage and frame it into the God-kind of marriage. By faith, you can build in your spouse everything that you want.

Sow into your wife's life by meeting her every need, and you will have the ideal woman you've desired all along. Sow into your husband's life by submitting to him and supporting him, and he will become the man of your dreams.

God's word will not fail you.

The Word is Profitable

The Bible says in Isaiah 48:17, ''... I am the Lord thy God which teacheth thee to profit, which leadeth thee by the way that thou shouldest go.''

The Word of the Lord will teach you how to profit, or prosper. The word prosper in the Greek means to have a good journey. God wants us to have a good journey in marriage--He wants us to prosper and be successful.

God's word imparts true wisdom and gives us the advantage in our marriages. Because most men and women have been trained by the world, we must retrain ourselves by reading and meditating on God's word; then we must put it into operation.

What prevents people from putting the Word of God into operation? It's either selfishness or the lack of a desire to practice Godly principles in their daily lives. We must choose which way we're going to go. We must never forget that we have been freewill moral agents. We have the freedom of choice.

We do not have to obey God, but life is so much better when we do. If you are a believer and you walk in disobedience to God, the Bible calls you a transgressor and says that your way is hard and you will not profit: ''...the way of transgressors is hard'' (Proverbs 13:15), and ''He that covereth his sins shall not prosper'' (Proverbs 28:13).

The Perfect Mate

... I am fearfully and wonderfully made.

Psalms 139:14

God knows you. He made you, and He knows you. If you are looking for a mate today, take time to ask God about it. He knows you spiritually, mentally, intellectually, emotionally, and physically. God will provide a mate to meet your needs. He made Eve especially for Adam, and He will make someone especially for you.

God made one woman specifically for one man. God is not going to send you a man or a woman who has affections for everybody else. Neither will He send you an indecisive man--someone who will date you for six months, then drop you like a hot potato.

Be aware that the devil will always send a package before the real thing comes along. So often people write me complaining that they married the wrong person. Unfortunately, they got excited and married the first person who came along.

Marriage is God's idea. Therefore, you must rely on God to send you the proper mate. God realized that Adam's singlehood was not good, and so He sent him the perfect mate. If you diligently seek God in selecting a marriage partner, He will send you the perfect mate, too.

Chapter Four

Selecting the Right Person

I want this book to minister to all the women whom God has redeemed--the wives, mothers, and single women--who are waiting on the Lord for the manifestation of their sacrificial lovers. I want you to know that God is preparing that particular man for you right now.

You may be wondering what he'll look like and how handsome he'll be. Or you may be curious about his occupation. In spite of all that is not known about your future mate, one thing is for certain: The man God is preparing for you is consecrated, dedicated, and holy. He speaks in tongues as the Spirit of God gives him utterance. He is a man of prayer. He is a man of praise and worship. He is a man who loves God with all of his heart, soul, mind, and strength. This is the type of man that God is preparing for all the women who are waiting upon Him for their mate.

Any man who approaches you and does not possess these characteristics is not sent from God. God always gives us His best. He doesn't send gigolos or backslidden men who, while they may appear to be saved because they speak in tongues and dance, follow their own will.

The man that God is preparing for you is a man who loves to fast and pray. He loves the things of God. I want to say to the women who have dedicated their hearts to God, that I know you've been struggling with the weakness and lack of commitment you see in the men of the church. But I want to destroy those oppressive thoughts and bring you to the place where you're standing solidly upon the promises of God, trusting in Him to bring your special person to you.

Many of you have a desire for a Godly mate; God is going to send him to you. Because of your hunger and thirst for God, through your consecration in prayer and fasting, and because your heart is for the ministry, God is going to send you the right mate. Whether he's a deacon, preacher, or pastor, he will be the right one for you. He will be someone who is on your level. God is not going to send you a "spiritual" gigolo who goes from church to church and woman to woman.

There are a lot of "church-wise" men in the church today; this is just like being "street-wise" in the world. These are the men who have been around the church long enough to look at a woman, size her up, and then move in for the "kill." They are used to reclining in the pew; you won't find them worshipping at the altar. God is not going to send you someone who runs from the altar, refuses to fast and pray, and fails to believe in Him. God can't use that person and neither can you!

If your husband is a product of your local church, he's going to look, think, and be dedicated to the things of God to the degree that the pastor is. Every church reproduces after its own kind.

The Bible explains that 400 men joined themselves to David and became his mighty men of valor. When these men first met David, they were poor, discouraged, and had no hope (1 Samuel 22:2). But through their association with David, they became like him--mighty men of valor (2 Samuel 17:8,10).

It is not my goal to produce weak-minded men. I want to produce men of strength, character, holiness, and godliness--mighty men of valor. I want to produce men who love God. Any man in my church who is truly born-again won't have babbling lips--he'll speak in tongues as the Spirit of God gives him utterance. Men who are birthed out of my ministry won't shuck or jive; nor will they walk by the road and pick flowers in a passive state. They'll understand that it's either holiness or hell!

Building Character

The cry of God in Jeremiah 5:1 remains the same today:

> *Run ye to and fro through the streets of Jerusalem, and see now, and know, and seek in the broad places thereof, if ye can find a man, if there be any that executeth judgment, that seeketh the truth; and I will pardon it.*

Men build men. People say that I'm hard, but I was produced by a man. I served a man of God who meant what he said. He had strength and character; therefore, he produced strong men.

There are people, even in the church, who have an idea of the God-kind of person they desire; but that idea is usually an ideal (their concept of perfection). When they find and marry that ''ideal'' person, they find out that what they have is an ordeal. Then after a while, they are looking for a new deal. But there is no place in God's plan for a new deal in marriage. You just have to work on your mate, through prayer, so that your spouse can become the ideal mate for you. And keep in mind that your ideal mate may not be what you had originally envisioned. Remember, you have to see marriage through the eyes of God and not through your carnal mind.

One day while seated with my wife at the kitchen table, I said to her, "Honey, as much as I think I know, I realize that I don't know anything." I felt as if I was just coming into an understanding of the basic principles of marriage, and we had been married 7 years.

I honestly feel like I've done my wife and family a disservice. I say this because after tediously studying for over 20 years, all of a sudden the light of revelation began to come.

So I began to express concern for those who don't study at all, for those who don't renew their minds, yet are attempting to manifest a successful marriage.

I believe that the reason I'm receiving revelation is simply because as a pastor, I have studied and come into powerful insight that is going to transform the lives of everyone who practices these principles.

God's Direction

> *Whoso findeth a wife findeth a good thing, and obtaineth favour of the LORD.*
>
> Proverbs 18:22

A lot of us have interpreted this Scripture to mean that we have to go out, on our own, and look for a wife. But to get the whole picture, you have to look at another Scripture that's found in Proverbs 3:5-6: "Trust in the Lord with all thine heart; and lean not unto thine own understanding. In all thy ways acknowledge him, and he shall direct thy paths." The Lord will direct you in finding that wife; He will put her right before you.

I remember when I first met my wife, Vickey. I went to a wedding which she also attended. It was during the reception that I first saw her--a pretty girl with long, pretty hair. I had already seen several other young ladies with long hair, but she was different.

At that time, the Coasters had produced a song entitled, ''With the Strings of my Heart.'' My heart went to beating, but it was no longer beating for me; it was beating for her. I started courting her, and asked her to marry me.

She initially had some objections to marrying me because I was a preacher and I was pastoring. She said, ''I don't want to be a pastor's wife; I'm not qualified.'' But I replied, ''Yes you are; if you love me, that's enough. I'll handle the church; you just love me and take care of our children.'' Then I asked her, ''What were you praying for?'' She answered, ''I just asked God for a man who loved Him, who was committed to Him, and who was full of the Holy Ghost; that's all I asked for. I had no idea you were coming; I really didn't want to marry a preacher.''

God is responsible to see to it that you have the person you need.

Know the Voice of God

One morning, before coming out to church, my wife and I were talking. She asked me, ''How will people know who their mates are?'' I responded, ''They will know if they know the voice of God. If they do not know God's voice, they will never know who God is bringing.'' Your emphasis should be on developing your relationship with God, not on finding the mate of your desires; God will take care of that.

Men, God wants you to have a helper. Genesis 2:18 says, ''...I will make him an help meet for him.'' God sees your lack and He will meet that need. Let Him bring your mate.

Because God saw that there was a lack in man and that it was not good, He said, ''I will fulfill it.'' So He took the rib out of Adam's side and fashioned a woman. But He didn't stop there--He brought her to Adam. God (not man) is the matchmaker.

Every church has its own matchmakers. Never listen to people who tell you, ''This person is for you.'' Never let your decision about whom to marry be made under the influence of another person's opinion. You must know God's voice for yourself.

I was once involved with an organization where the pastors went around saying, ''You are made for this person. Come on--we're going to have a marriage!''

Marrying a person because someone else decides you should, is not the way God brings believers together. Some of these ''chosen'' people aren't even saved. And if you want to live in hell on earth, marry someone that you only ''think'' is saved.

God formed Eve and brought her to Adam. There were certain characteristics which Adam needed from Eve. She was perfectly suited to him intellectually, emotionally, physically, and most importantly, spiritually. God saw the lack, met the need by bringing the woman to Adam, then gave her away. Make sure you get the person God is giving to you.

No Human Movement

Genesis 2:21 says, ''God caused a deep sleep to fall upon Adam.'' While Adam was asleep, there was no movement from him. Adam was totally unaware of what God was doing because he was asleep. He was in a state of helpessness.

Whether you are married, single, separated, or divorced, when you are waiting for God to move in the area of companionship, there can be no human movement.

The problem with most people in the church today is that they have not come to the place where they helplessly throw themselves on the mercy of God. Adam had a need, but he did not know what he needed. When it comes to something as important as selecting an individual to spend the rest of your life with, you do not want to take a chance by relying upon your own judgement. You don't know what you need! There was no movement with Adam; it was totally in the hands of God.

Single believers need to understand how God works. It is not known how long Adam slept, or how long he was helpless. Singles, while you are waiting, helpless, God is making that man or woman that you need. Time is not the issue. He is fashioning that person for you right now, and in His appointed time, which is the perfect time, God will put that person before you.

God brought Eve to Adam. She was perfect for him. Whomever your wife or husband is, God will also bring that perfect person to you.

Be Equally Yoked

Be ye not unequally yoked together with unbelievers: for what fellowship hath righteousness with unrighteousness? and what communion hath light with darkness?

And what concord hath Christ with Belial? or what part hath he that believeth with an infidel?

And what agreement hath the temple of God with

idols? for ye are the temple of the living God; as God hath said, I will dwell in them, and walk in them; and I will be their God, and they shall be my people.

Wherefore come out from among them, and be ye separate, saith the Lord, and touch not the unclean thing; and I will receive you,

And will be a Father unto you, and ye shall be my sons and daughters, saith the Lord Almighty.

2 Corinthians 6:14-18

In most of the New Testament Scriptures, the word ''yoked'' refers to marriage. God has gone on record as saying, ''Be not married to unbelievers.'' (And it should be noted that all of the marital advice given to us by the Apostle Paul in the book of Ephesians is based upon the assumption that both of the marriage partners are saved; Paul is not addressing the unsaved. The first step for unbelievers is salvation. Then God can minister to their marriage through His word.)

Even though you should not consider marrying an unbeliever, I have heard all sorts of stories about God leading people to marry unbelievers. I rebuke such thinking! God will never lead you to an unbeliever. However, if you associate regularly with unbelievers, your emotions are going to overrule your better judgment. And once you get emotionally involved with a person, you will find a way to justify why you should marry that person. It is very difficult to see clearly once your emotions are involved; you will begin making ''emotional'' decisions instead of ones based upon your better judgment. You will forget that God said you will become unequally yoked if you marry an unbeliever.

I'd like to share a principle with you: People tend to marry among those with whom they most frequently associate. This may be hard to accept, but it's true. And if you make the choice to live by it, you will be spared the pain that comes when you marry the wrong person.

The reason most women consider marrying unsaved men (and women have more problems with this than men) is because there is a shortage of men; there's a shortage of men in the world, and an even greater one in the church. Women, if you heed my warning, it will save you many nights of crying: Don't become friends with an unsaved man! I'll go a step further: Don't consider marrying a man who has only recently been born-again. Take time to study him. See whether or not he hangs around the altar. Thoroughly examine his commitment to God.

If a brother has not been saved for two or three years, you shouldn't even be bothered with him. Why that long? Because if he hasn't been saved for two or three years, he hasn't gone through enough tests. When you're newly born-again, your mind is not yet renewed--you still possess the former thinking of the world. The testing that believers go through is a process by which our minds are renewed or regenerated. You do not want a mate with an unregenerated mind. It will only lead to heartache.

The sisters need to be aware that some of the things they do only encourage these young brothers to continue thinking of themselves as Don Juans or Romeos. Some of these brothers could have been losers in the world, but then they get saved, and overnight they become Don Juans because so many of the sisters are pursuing them. Their minds are not yet renewed and they need to be left alone to sit under the word of God, so a transformation can begin to take place in their lives. They'll be ready for the sisters later, but not when they're first saved. If you get one of these brothers at the state when he doesn't yet have the mind of Christ, saying that God put you two together, and you marry him, six months down the road he may not even want to come to church. When he's no longer interested in the things of God, your heartache will begin.

If you want a good Bible lesson on this, read the fourth chapter of the Gospel of Mark. When the sower sows the word, immediately the devil comes to steal that word. The parable describes the various types of ground where the word is sown. You will understand why it is so necessary for you to stand back and observe the individual you are interested in. Watch how he matures in God. God may decide to speak a word to you concerning the person being your mate, but don't get in a hurry and reveal it to him. Don't say, ''You know God put us together; I'm praying for you.'' Just keep it to yourself and pray.

Hard to Get

The principle in the world of ''playing hard to get'' is the same in the church--men do not value that which comes too easily. Men, saved or unsaved, do not value a woman who is too easy to get. Women should have dignity, character, and stability. Women are not to be pursuers; they are to be pursued. If a man doesn't pursue you before you are married, he will not pursue you afterwards. Sadly, what he will tell you then is, ''What do you want? I didn't do that before I married you. Change? Who me? What's wrong with me? I was good enough for you when I married you.'' These are not words you want to hear. If a man will not pursue you, he is not the man God has sent to you.

When a man has to pursue you in order to win you, you are sending him a message that you are somebody special, and you expect him to treat you accordingly. If you conduct yourself like a queen during the courtship, he will continue to treat you like royalty after he marries you. Most women want to be treated like queens, but the problem is they didn't act like queens when they were courting.

In the years that I've been pastoring, I've discovered that about ninety-nine percent of the problems I have to deal with in counseling are domestic-related. This underscores the importance of the man and woman understanding and moving in their proper roles in courtship and marriage. If the home-life of the saints gets straightened out, we'll have a better church.

No Fellowship with Darkness

> *...what fellowship hath righteousness with unrighteousness? and what communion hath light with darkness?*

> 2 Corinthians 6:14

God will NEVER join a saved person to an unsaved person in marriage. If God's joining two people, they have to be Spirit-filled. If a man or woman does not meet God's requirements, don't date them. And to elaborate a little further on that point, don't continue to date someone you're not considering for marriage.

In a relationship, through the course of the different activities we engage in--going out to eat, going for a car ride, visiting amusement parks, and other types of outings--bonding takes place; this is inevitable because it's the way God made us. Sharing similar experiences and talking together about different things brings a man and woman closer together. This is primarily a word to the sisters: Don't allow anyone to monopolize your time if he's not talking about marriage. You'll only get hurt.

Sisters, when you allow a man to dominate or control your time you are saying, "I'm interested." If you're not interested, don't lead him on. Instead, tell him, "I like you and you're a nice friend, but you're not what God is sending me so there's no sense in us going on like this."

The Carnal Saint

You can be a Christian and yet walk in darkness. Have you ever heard of a carnal saint? A carnal saint is a believer who is dead while he lives: "For to be carnally minded is death...Because the carnal mind is enmity against God: for it is not subject to the law of God, neither indeed can be" (Romans 8:6-7).

To be carnally minded is death. That is why we also caution all women not to marry a believer whom they haven't seen in several years. You need to see what he's going through as well as what type of character he possesses. You don't want to marry a dead believer.

You may say, "But he speaks in tongues...." Well, I've heard a lot of men speak in tongues and then I've watched them do all sorts of ungodly things. Most of these men get saved and come to church for the sole reason of catching some woman. Their motive is impure and after a while the true intention on their heart will show. The aftermath of these types of situations is very sad: six months later, these men won't even come to church. Then I have to meet with the heartbroken wives. But if they had just read their Bible, they wouldn't have to experience such disappointment.

If a man says he is Spirit-filled and walks in darkness, do not be deceived into thinking you can make him see the light. The only person who can make such a man see the light is the Spirit of God.

The Bible says that "the tree is known by his fruit" (Matthew 12:33). It doesn't take long to discern where a person's heart is, for "out of the abundance of the heart the mouth speaketh" (Matthew 12:34). If you take time to really listen to a person's conversation, examine their lifestyle, and the friends with whom they associate, then you can determine whether they are truly from God. Don't ignore the fruit a person produces: does it lead to righteousness or unrighteousness?

Chapter Five

The Spirit-Led Marriage

And be not drunk with wine, wherein is excess; but be filled with the Spirit;

Speaking to yourselves in psalms and hymns and spiritual songs, singing and making melody in your heart to the Lord;

Giving thanks always for all things unto God and the Father in the name of our Lord Jesus Christ....

Ephesians 5:18-20

Through the mouth of the Apostle Paul, the apostle to the Gentiles, our roles have been defined. Paul was saying, ''Be stimulated and come under the control and influence of the Holy Spirit.'' To have God's best, to have the ideal God-kind of marriage, you need to be filled with and continuously under the influence of the Holy Spirit.

In order to have a Holy Spirit-led marriage, the Holy

Spirit must be in control of your life. You must constantly yield to and continuously be filled with the Holy Spirit in order for Him to lead you and have control of your life. Because you are Spirit-filled and speak with other tongues as the Spirit of God gives you utterance, you must learn how to follow the Holy Spirit. Don't try to lead Him; He will not take orders from you.

The Holy Spirit was sent to help and bless you. He was sent to lead you, not to follow you. The Holy Spirit wants to do something great for you, but you must first yield to Him. If you don't yield to Him, He cannot bless you. He is the Helper who is called alongside of you. He's not called to do it all; He comes to help or assist you. He is called to be an advocate for you. He is called to strengthen and stand by you. If you understand His functions, then He will aid you in the things of God. He is also the Spirit of truth who comes to reveal truth unto you.

As the Holy Spirit reveals truth to you and begins to gain influence over your life, you will learn to praise, honor, worship, and glorify God in all things. This is very important for the well-being of your marriage. Most people praise and worship God while everything is going well, but when in the midst of trials and tribulations they stop. That's when you need to praise God more! When the devil applies pressure, instead of bending under his attack, you need to resist him by applying your own pressure through praising and worshipping God. I guarantee you he will flee every time (James 4:7).

We all have something to praise God for. The chief reason to lift your hands and praise God is for salvation. If your name is written in the Lamb's book of life, no matter what happens, Jesus is still yours.

Learn to praise God for what you have. Set an example in your marriage, and in your household. I have so much to be

thankful for. When I think about what God has done for me--
joy in my soul, peace in my mind, a healthy body, a lovely wife
and family, clothes on my back, food on my table, a place to
lay my head--I know I have something to thank Him for! But
I've also learned to thank God for the tests and trials, for it's
in the tests and trials that God reveals Himself to me; and I'm
getting to know Him better.

Ungodly Counsel

> *Blessed is the man that walketh not in the counsel*
> *of the ungodly....*

> Psalms 1:1

Don't assume that everyone who speaks in tongues is
speaking under the influence of the Holy Spirit. All over the
world there are "tongue-talking" people in Spirit-filled churches
who don't even know God. They wouldn't recognize God if
He appeared in their midst. In fact, they'd probably kick Him
out!

I'm reminded of a story about a little southern lady
who went to visit a local church one day. Now this woman was
used to praising God, and so while the preacher was preaching, she said, "Hallelujah!" A hundred heads turned to look
at her. The preacher continued preaching and she spoke out
again saying, "Thank you Jesus!" The people turned around
again. By this time the preacher was fed up, too. He looked
over to the deacons as if to say, "Get rid of that woman!"

When they got back to where she was sitting, she said,
"Thank you Lord," and stood up. The deacons said, "Lady,
you've got to be quiet; we don't do that here." And this little
Spirit-filled woman said, "I can't be quiet; I have the Holy

Ghost!'' One of the deacons replied, ''Well, you may have the Holy Ghost, but you didn't get it here.'' And the sad truth was that the Holy Spirit hadn't been in that church for a very long time. Their counsel was ungodly because God was not in their midst.

Godly Counsel

Godly counsel is vitally important for a good marriage. God wants you to walk in godly counsel; He doesn't want you to walk in darkness. You must be aware that everyone who claims to speak in the name of the Lord is not moving by His Spirit. There are people who dance, speak in tongues, and prophesy, but not under the influence of the Holy Spirit. Do not be deceived. Following the wrong advice will wreak havoc in your marriage.

In The Amplified Bible, Psalms 1:1-3 reads this way:

> *Blessed--happy, fortunate, prosperous and enviable--is the man who walks and lives not in the counsel of the ungodly [following their advice, their plans and purposes], nor stands [submissive and inactive] in the path where sinners walk, nor sits down [to relax and rest] where the scornful [and the mocker] gather. But his delight and desire are in the law of the Lord, and on His law-- the precepts, the instructions, the teachings of God--he habitually meditates [ponders and studies] by day and by night. And he shall be like a tree firmly planted [and tended] by the streams of water, ready to bring forth his fruit in its season; his leaf also shall not fade or wither, and everything he does shall prosper [and come to maturity].*

The word ''blessed'' in the Hebrew means ''happy.'' The happy man, the prosperous man, is the man who first delights himself in the law of the Lord. He must meditate on the word of God, rolling it over and over in his mind. He must insert himself in the Scriptures and actually become a doer of the word. The Bible says that after you do these things, you will be blessed (happy).

All of our lives, we've been programmed with ungodly advice by the god of this world, Satan. The Bible says, ''... the whole world lieth in wickedness'' (1 John 5:19). But then we get saved, we join a local assembly, and we begin to have our minds washed from this ungodly advice. As our minds are washed and cleansed by the word of God, our lives are transformed. As a direct result of this transformation, we move from an unhappy, cursed state to a happy, blessed state. It is within this happy, blessed state that we can bring the most to a marriage.

By reasoning, sometimes because of a lack of knowledge and sometimes by choice (because we are free-moral agents), some people choose to cling to the preconceived thoughts and ideas that have been programmed into us by the world; they do not reprogram themselves with the word of God.

But God is moving today by His Spirit. God is building an end-time army and purging His church. The Bible says, ''For the time is come that judgment must begin at the house of God...'' (1 Peter 4:17).

Especially in this latter day, there will always be people who are willing to give you ungodly counsel. The only way you will be able to tell the difference between godly and ungodly counsel is by studying God's word. Don't be deceived into allowing someone else to study for you; we have to study and pray for ourselves (2 Timothy 2:15).

Infilling of the Holy Spirit

> *And when the day of Pentecost was fully come, they were all with one accord in one place.*
>
> *And suddenly there came a sound from heaven as of a rushing mighty wind, and it filled all the house where they were sitting.*
>
> *And there appeared unto them cloven tongues like as of fire, and it sat upon each of them.*
>
> *And they were all filled with the Holy Ghost, and began to speak with other tongues, as the Spirit gave them utterance.*

Acts 2:1-4

The initial sign that you have been baptized by the Holy Spirit is that you will speak with other tongues as the Spirit of God gives you utterance. Unfortunately, there is an erroneous teaching in the body of Christ concerning this baptism.

People have said that once you receive the initial sign you never have to pray in the Holy Spirit again. That's incorrect. The truth is, speaking with other tongues is not a one-time experience because if you are going to remain full of the Holy Spirit, you must continue to pray in tongues on a regular basis.

There is a difference between the initial baptism of the Holy Spirit and continuously being filled with the Holy Spirit. There are a lot of people who have been baptized with the Holy Spirit but who are no longer filled with Him. You have to constantly stay filled with the Holy Ghost.

Staying Filled

He that believeth on me, as the scripture hath said, out of his belly shall flow rivers of living water.

(But this spake he of the Spirit, which they that believe on him should receive)....

John 7:38-39

At the Straight Gate Church, we teach a principle on praying in the Spirit: Every believer who has been baptized with the Holy Spirit should pray at least one hour a day in the Spirit. If you follow that, you will continually stay filled with the Holy Ghost.

If you are going to have the ideal marriage (according to God's design for you) you must stay full of the Holy Ghost. Rejoicing in the Lord is great--running around and dancing up and down the church aisles--but it is no indication that you are filled with the Holy Ghost. Those are outward manifestations that could be coming from the emotional or psychological parts of your inner man.

There are genuine outward expressions when one is overcome by the Holy Ghost. For instance, 1 Kings 8:10-11 says, ''And it came to pass, when the priests were come out of the holy place, that the cloud filled the house of the Lord, So that the priests could not stand to minister because of the cloud: for the glory of the Lord had filled the house of the Lord.'' They were so overcome by the presence of God that they couldn't even stand!

There is a time in church services when the Holy Ghost enters in and you can't go any further in the service; so you just worship Him. You let God do whatever He wants to do, because He has filled the place.

God wants to have the same type of control in your marriage. If you are going to have the ideal marriage, you must stay full of the Holy Ghost; you must remain under the control of and stimulated by the Holy Spirit. Receiving from God through His Spirit will result in stronger marriages; the Holy Spirit can heal your marriage.

Read Acts, chapter four, to revive your thinking about being filled with the Holy Ghost. In order for God to work through us the way He wants to, we need to be continuously filled with the Holy Ghost. When Jesus ministered to the multitiudes, in the fifth chapter of Mark, virtue had gone out of Him. Jesus had to go back to the Father for a refilling--He needed to replenish that which He'd given.

The way to stay full of the Holy Spirit is to stay before the Lord. If you want to have the God-kind of marriage, you must remain full of the Holy Ghost. Having the God-kind of marriage is not predicated upon your intellectualism or your ability; it is predicated upon the Spirit of the Living God's ability. This is why we must stay filled--so God has a channel (us) to flow into and through to accomplish His will.

When I visited Jerusalem, I stood in awe when I saw the temple, proclaiming, ''What a mighty God we serve!'' Then the Holy Spirit spoke to me, saying, ''But the temple was closed.'' And I was reminded of the words of Jesus: ''... the hour cometh, when ye shall neither in this mountain, nor yet at Jerusalem, worship the Father'' (John 4:21). Jesus went on to say, ''... when he, the Spirit of truth, is come, he will guide you into all truth ...'' (John 6:13).

God is looking for a people who will worship Him from their heart. I stood in awe when I saw the temple, yet God had not lived there for many years. Today, you and I have become the temple of the living God. And it's easy to be stimulated by the Spirit of God if He's living within you. When you pray in the Holy Ghost, you stimulate, build up, and charge yourself. You'll become filled with the Holy Ghost, not just baptized with Him, and overflowing with the power of the mighty God.

Walking with God

When you walk with God, according to His laws and precepts, not only will you prosper, but your marriage will prosper as well. Right living alone will cause you to prosper, because holiness is profitable (1 Timothy 4:8).

There was a time on the face of the earth when no one walked with God. Then came a man named Enoch (Genesis 5:22-24). As Enoch continued to walk with God, he became very special to God. I imagine their conversation went something like this: God said, ''Enoch, turn around and look where you are; your house is way back over there.'' And Enoch replied, ''That's a long walk.'' So God said, ''But there's a place over here that's closer; it's my house. You're too close to my house to go back. Come and go with me.'' And the Bible says, ''... and he (Enoch) was not; for God took him.''

God translated Enoch because of his life which had gone up before God as a memorial. When you walk with God revelation knowledge comes, your faith increases, and a change in your life takes place. God-ordained things begin to happen when you walk with God. A perfect example of this is found in the story of Elisha.

Elisha was plowing the fields when Elijah passed and threw his mantle upon him (1 Kings 19:19). There's something about the mantle of God that once it touches you, you're never the same. Elisha knew that in the casting of the mantle upon his life, God had called him. Yet that was not enough. The Bible says, ''For many are called, but few are chosen'' (Matthew 22:14). Following the call, Elisha had a decision to make.

Many people have been called, but have not responded. Even though your response doesn't change God's mind about you (Romans 11:29), it will affect the outcome. The response of Elisha and Peter to the call of God on their lives was distinctly different. Elisha responded by having a party; he was glad to be called into the service of the Lord. Peter, on the other hand, only put his boat up for a season. In other words, while Elisha destroyed the instruments of his livelihood (1 Kings 19:20-21) Peter made preparation for failure. I imagine him thinking, ''I'll just put the boat up for a while. If need be, I'll come back and pick it up later. I can always return to my job as a fisherman if this thing with Jesus doesn't work out.''

Peter expected failure, so he failed. Elisha made no preparation for failure; he had nothing to go back to when he began to walk with the prophet. When Elisha requested a double portion of Elijah's spirit (anointing), Elijah replied, ''Thou hast asked a hard thing'' (2 Kings 2:10). But because he was willing to tarry or wait on Elijah, Elisha received his petition.

There are many more people to whom God desires to give His best, but they are not willing to wait on it. They are not willing to go after it with persistence. Prior to Elijah's being caught away by a whirlwind, the only one known to have left the earth alive was Enoch. But that didn't stop Elisha from receiving the revelation: 2 Kings 2:11-12 says, ''And it came to pass, as they still went on, and talked, that, behold, there appeared a chariot of fire, and horses of fire, and parted them both asunder; and Elijah went up by a whirlwind into heaven. And Elisha saw it ....'' When the chariot began to ascend back up into heaven, Elijah still had the mantle. It appeared as if Elijah was going to take the mantle to heaven. But that didn't stop Elisha. He remembered the covenant, " ... if thou see me when I am taken from thee, it shall be so unto thee ...," and he kept his eyes on Elijah (verse 10). He was not disappointed.

Let me paraphrase what I believe happened in Elisha's case. I believe that the first time Elisha cried out to Elijah, Elijah heard him. But being so excited about what was happening, Elijah did not respond to Elisha's cry. Elisha cried loudly for his master; but the further away someone gets, the harder it becomes for them to hear. I believe that when the chariot was almost out of sight, Elijah heard Elisha's cry and said, "Oh, I did promise something to that young man." He then reached over in the chariot and dropped down the mantle.

Some of you do not have your eyes on the man of God (the pastor) in your life. There may be some members in your local assembly who try to covet his role, but there is only one God-appointed under-shepherd in your assembly. There is only one that speaks by revelation, so keep your eyes on him. Just as in the case of Elijah and Elisha, God has given a revelation to the man of God in your life. But be aware that there are people who, because of their own ignorance and inability to commit to the things of God, are out to destroy the pastor's vision. Do not be deceived by them!

God has given a revelation to His church on the marriage covenant. God intends for His church to have the strongest marriages in the earth. But like Elisha, you must be willing to pay the price.

In your walk with God, if you learn how to open your spiritual ears and allow the Holy Spirit to speak to you, you will receive from God every time.

Chapter Six

The Sexual Relationship

*Marriage is honourable in all, and the bed undefiled:
but whoremongers and adulterers God will judge.*

Hebrews 13:4

The Bible teaches emphatically that the intimate-sexual relationship is only to be between a husband and wife. Yet many people are operating with worldly knowledge in the area of sexual relationships. They are relying on what they learned in the streets, not realizing the Bible is full of information on this topic.

In Hebrews 13:4, the Scripture not only states that the whoremongers and adulterers will be judged, but more emphatically that "God will judge." God is so protective of the marriage covenant that when people step outside of it by committing adultery, God personally hands down judgement. It is never God's will that a marriage get to the point of adultery, but if it does, God will uphold what is right. The person who steps outside of the marriage covenant will come under His judgement.

The intimate-sexual relationship is confined to marriage. God set the terms for marriage and decreed that the sexual union is to be between a husband and wife. The highest fulfillment in this intimate-sexual relationship comes when the couple understands this spiritual principle. The intimate-sexual relationship comes because you care. It comes when you show warmth, appreciation, love, and respect; these qualities are spiritual. In the absence of these, sex becomes just a mechanical act and the real enjoyment is missing. It is a waste to just have sex without the spiritual involvement; that's where most husbands miss it.

It is impossible for a woman to completely give herself physically to her husband when he does not love her emotionally. Brethren, God holds you responsible for your home. It is your job to love your wife, to cherish her, to honor her, and to respect her. How is it that you want to be treated like a king, yet you treat her like dirt? If you are a king, that makes her a queen. She should look like you look and be taken care of like you take care of yourself.

Men must love and respect their wives. Both husband and wife should look good. The husband should not go out and buy a fully accessorized, expensive suit and allow his wife to look ill-cared for. The Bible says, ''For no man ever yet hated his own flesh; but nourisheth and cherisheth it, even as the Lord the church'' (Ephesians 5:29). Take care of your wife; make her look good. In fact, adorn her with fine clothing first.

A husband should cherish his wife and not put her down or be critical. Never discuss with others what goes on in your house. If you find you need to seek marital counseling, make sure both of you go together. It is a waste of time to speak with only one marital partner at a time because each person usually sees the situation differently. And finally, if the two of you feel you can discuss your circumstances in front of your pastor, then you should be able to sit down as two intelligent people and discuss it in the privacy of your home. I think you will find that it is best to work your problems out between yourselves.

Fornication and Adultery

"Have you two been together sexually?"

"No."

"My reason for asking you this is because marriage is not a fleshly covenant; it is a spiritual covenant."

This dialogue represents part of the first discussion I have with two people who are seeking to enter into the marriage covenant. Marriage is not a fleshly covenant; it is spiritual. It is vitally important that the man and woman understand this. When I ask them if they've been together, it is for the purpose of seeing if they hear God's voice clearly. God will NEVER tell two people to try out sex before they marry. The principle being that, that which is of the flesh produces flesh, and that which is of the spirit produces spirit. God is not promoting the flesh; He's promoting His Spirit.

So if you believe that God is bringing the two of you together, you do not want to mess it up. If you do commit fornication, you're asking for trouble. What often happens is that after marriage, when you have one of those big arguments (that you never thought you'd have), the wife finds herself saying, "It wasn't God's will for us to be married anyway; you violated me!" The devil will then have grounds in your life to torment you in your mind. If given half a chance, he will convince you that you did indeed marry the wrong person; this is a sorry state to be in. But you can avoid all that by learning the correct way to enter into the marriage covenant.

You must be aware that fornication is not simply the act of sexual intercourse; fornication is any sexual impurity. If a woman allows a man to move his hands all over her body, that's fornication. On some of those hot petting nights when your passions get aroused and the man's hands start to roam, and you ignore the voice inside you that's saying, "Stop!" that's fornication.

I don't care who you are or what position you hold in the church, this type of behavior is fornication. I was traveling with a pastor-friend of mine one day. While on the road, we began to discuss how he met his wife. While he was talking about her being so spiritual and dedicated to the things of God, he suddenly said, "She was just as saved as she could be. After I took her clothes off (this occurred prior to their marriage), she still wouldn't allow me to complete the act." He almost had an accident when I replied, "That's fornication!" He didn't believe it was.

And there are a lot of people today who do not want to admit what the real definition of fornication is. Yet the Bible says in Proverbs 6:27, "Can a man take fire in his bosom, and his clothes not be burned?" This means, how can you stir up passion and it not affect you? And Jesus said, " ... whosoever looketh on a woman to lust after her hath committed adultery [which is fornication] with her already in his heart" (Matthew 5:28). When single people say, "Do not get married; just do what you want," that's fornication. And without a doubt, God will judge it.

Another form of sexual immorality (which is fornication) is homosexuality. Beastiality, when a person lies with an animal, is also fornication. These acts are reprehensible to God and He will judge them. You must be aware that if you are in a situation where your spouse is involved in sexual immorality of any type, God is on your side; He is going to do something about what your partner is doing. Your spouse is not just sinning against you, but against God. Through His word, God has already declared that the man or woman who commits adultery is without understanding: "But whoso committeth adultery with a woman lacketh understanding: he that doeth it destroyeth his own soul" (Proverbs 6:32).

An adulterer is not a person who has it all together, like the world would have us believe. The world presents television shows and movies which depict fornication and adultery in a very glamorized state. These programs glorify sin to make the star of the show look like the all-knowing good guy. But it doesn't matter how it's packaged--sexual immorality is still wrong.

Sexual sins bring shame and are as "rottenness in the bones" (Proverbs 12:4). The Apostle Paul goes on to say, "Know ye not that the unrighteous shall not inherit the kingdom of God? Be not deceived: neither fornicators, nor idolaters, nor adulterers, nor effeminate, nor abusers of themselves with mankind ... shall inherit the kingdom of God" (1 Corinthians 6:9-10).

When you become a fornicator or adulterer, you forfeit your right to enter heaven. If you've ever thought about looking at a woman other than your wife, you'd better consider the consequences as found in God's word; that should change your mind. The price you will have to pay is too high, so you don't want to be moved by your feelings alone. There are going to be a lot of people in hell who operated in their feelings. They will have all eternity to remember that they said, "I couldn't help myself."

Hell will not be a playground; there won't be any joy there. Many people are playing games right now with the things of God because they don't know any better. We've all come from families and backgrounds where immorality was prevalent; it was a way of life. But now that we're members of Christ's church, having been translated from the kingdom of darkness into the kingdom of light, we must learn a better way.

The Temple of God

> *I beseech you therefore, brethren, by the mercies of God, that ye present your bodies a living sacrifice, holy, acceptable unto God, which is your reasonable service.*
>
> *And be not conformed to this world: but be ye transformed by the renewing of your mind, that ye may prove what is that good, and acceptable, and perfect, will of God.*
>
> Romans 12:1-2

Your body is the temple of God; God dwells in you. You become responsible for the temple. The Bible says, "If any man defile the temple of God, him shall God destroy; for the temple of God is holy, which temple ye are" (1 Corinthians 3:17). It goes on to say, "Flee fornication. Every sin that a man doeth is without the body; but he that committeth fornication sinneth against his own body" (1 Corinthians 6:18).

Some of you are playing with fire; and the truth is, you cannot get away with it. You may not get caught today, tomorrow, or even next year, but sooner or later, your deeds will be revealed. The Bible says that if you continue to destroy your body with sexual sins, the judgement of God will come upon you (1 Corinthians 3:17).

There is no place in the world where you can go to hide from God. Regardless of how you try to cover yourself, God will find you. You may try to hide through justifying your actions by saying, "My wife isn't this ..." and "My husband isn't that ...," but God is saying, "It's still wrong!" You are the temple of God and when you cohabit with a person outside of marriage, God calls it spiritual adultery. So when your body starts deteriorating, don't call the pastor or anyone else. No one can get you straight but you. You have an internal conflict that you must resolve.

There is a principle I'd like to share with you. The Apostle Paul said, in 1 Corinthians 9:27, "... I keep under my body, and bring it into subjection ...." God honors only that which is placed on His altar. You will not receive wisdom, revelation, and understanding from God, nor will your mind be renewed, until you present your body as a living sacrifice. If you don't put your body on the altar and allow the fire of the Holy Ghost to sanctify you through the consuming of the lust of the flesh, your mind will never be renewed. God wants your body first; wisdom, revelation, and understanding will follow.

Mutual Consent

Now concerning the things whereof ye wrote unto me: It is good for a man not to touch a woman.

Nevertheless, to avoid fornication, let every man have his own wife, and let every woman have her own husband.

Let the husband render unto the wife due benevo-

lence: and likewise also the wife unto the husband.

The wife hath not power of her own body, but the husband: and likewise also the husband hath not power of his own body, but the wife.

Defraud ye not one the other, except it be with consent for a time, that ye may give yourselves to fasting and prayer; and come together again, that Satan tempt you not for your incontinency.

1 Corinthians 7:1-5

In the first six chapters of the book of First Corinthians, Paul is responding to some questions that had been presented to him by the house of Chloe. This particular passage of Scripture is dealing with the need for people to be married and the mutual consent required to make that marriage work.

Paul is saying that, whether you are male or female, in order to avoid fornication or sexual sins, if you are the norm (and not the exception), you need to be married. According to Paul, if you defraud (which means to withhold unlawfully what rightfully belongs to another) each other, you are asking for trouble. You talk about opening a door for the devil--that will do it!

Let's take fasting for an example. I've heard people say they've fasted forty days because the Lord led them to. But I'm telling you that if you fast forty days, two weeks, or even one day without your mate's permission, you are not fasting according to the will of God. The Bible teaches us to do everything decently and in order (1 Corinthians 14:40). Therefore, if you decide to fast and abstain from sex without your spouse's permission, you are out of order and in violation of

Scriptures. You cannot be blessed that way; God will not honor your sacrifice.

I remember an incident that occurred some years ago. A woman stood up in church and said, "I fasted from sex for 21 days." The next week her husband left her. Now, I'm not saying that her fasting was the reason her husband left her, but I am saying that in those 21 days of consecration and dedication she surely should have received a word from the Lord; otherwise, what was she fasting for? We must be sure that what we do falls within the order of God's word.

When someone comes to me for counseling and says, "The Lord told me ...," I don't doubt what they're saying; that's between them and God. What I do question, however, is their knowledge of the Scriptures. God will never say anything that contradicts His word. And God is very specific regarding the guidelines for marriage.

When you marry, your body no longer belongs to you-- you are given (to one another) in marriage. Now, you are aware that your body first belongs to the Lord--it is His temple. But secondly, it becomes the property of your spouse-- you become one flesh. The only lawful reason, according to God's word, for withholding intimate-sexual relations from one another is for the purpose of fasting and praying; and this is to be done by agreement only. One last word of caution: Wives, do not use your bodies to train your husbands; husbands, do not use your bodies to punish your wives. God has a better way.

The Eunuch

> *For I would that all men were even as I myself.*
> *But every man hath his proper gift of God, one*
> *after this manner, and another after that.*

1 Corinthians 7:7

The Apostle Paul, who was unmarried, was writing about the state of the eunuch, which he considered to be a special gift from God. Being a eunuch is an accepted call, but it is not the usual or normal call, because God has given most men and women a desire to be married.

But a eunuch has no need to marry--he has no desire (in any way) for a mate. It is a very unique call. A eunuch does not want to be single today, and tomorrow decides he needs a mate. A true eunuch never needs to be united in marriage. He is perfectly content to serve God in his singleness.

If a eunuch marries, he's in for trouble because he's of that group of people that should not marry. If the eunuch marries, he (or she) will miss his calling. Eunuchs are called to serve God apart from the marital union; what marriage has to offer, they have no need (or desire) for.

On the other hand, there are those within the church who are married but are yet trying to live as eunuchs for the "kingdom's sake." This causes a lot of problems. Being a eunuch is an ordained gift from God. In the same way that eunuchs shouldn't marry, married people should not attempt to live as eunuchs. You don't marry and then decide you want to serve God as a single person; you should make that decision before you marry.

If a single person is attempting to live as a eunuch although he's not really one, he's going to have a problem. Single people who realize that they are not eunuchs, should earnestly seek the Lord for a mate. Otherwise, you are setting yourself up to commit fornication.

I know there are many people who do not agree with me on this, but I'm taking the Apostle Paul's stance. He said, "You will not have problems in the flesh if you have a husband or a wife." His reason for saying this is because we are made with the desire to be touched, held, and told nice things. It's not wrong to desire a mate.

Some people who have been in the church all their lives are still holding on to the ''puritan'' concept. Don't be deceived by such nonsense. The desires that men and women have for one another are normal and ordained of God. The initmate personal relationship that God has designed for the human family is not dirty--it's clean, pure, wholesome, and spiritual. But God only permits such desires to be fulfilled within the marital union. And He's also saying that in the absence of these desires, for those who are called to be eunuchs, you can serve Him just as well within the unique gift of your calling. Allow the Lord to meet your needs. Whether in marriage or out, He is able.

Chapter Seven

The Wife's Role

Be ye followers of me, even as I also am of Christ.

Now I praise you, brethren, that ye remember me in all things, and keep the ordinances, as I delivered them to you.

But I would have you know, that the head of every man is Christ; and the head of the woman is the man; and the head of Christ is God.

Every man praying or prophesying, having his head covered, dishonoureth his head.

But every woman that prayeth or prophesieth with her head uncovered dishonoureth her head: for that is even all one as if she were shaven.

For if the woman be not covered, let her also be shorn: but if it be a shame for a woman to be shorn or shaven, let her be covered.

For a man indeed ought not to cover his head, forasmuch as he is the image and glory of God: but the woman is the glory of the man. For the man is not of the woman; but the woman of the man.

1 Corinthians 11:1-7

In writing to the Corinthians, a Spirit-filled church, the Apostle Paul was attempting to establish some guidelines for the roles of men and women in the church. Today, God is still endeavoring to bring His people to the proper understanding of their roles.

When we are saved, we bring the hostility or carnal thinking that we held in the world into the church. Most of us come from homes that have never been properly established, homes where godly examples of husbands and wives were never displayed. While this places us at a disadvantage, there is hope: the hope is in God's word. Through His word, God can change our thinking and lead us into a better way--His way.

We need to examine the word of God, embrace it and allow it to separate us from our preconceived thoughts and ideas. Jesus said, "And ye shall know the truth, and the truth shall make you free" (John 8:32). The word of God will set you free in every area of your life.

In this text, Paul is saying that the man is created in the image of God. The Greek meaning for image is "exact duplicate, nothing varying." So this means that the man is an exact duplicate of God--His image and His glory. The woman, on the other hand, is the glory of the man. God does not look down upon women; that is not why He put this Scripture in the Bible. Conversely, He highly esteems women and desires that they would move in the fullness of their womanhood. That can only happen when both men and women understand their place and purpose in God's plan.

Paul was dealing with a culture, using truth that was established by God. He had to approach the Corinthians in a manner that they could identify with. What he said must be interpreted in the context in which it was written.

It's important to understand why God created Eve. In the beginning, when man had continuous unbroken fellowship with God, God determined that something was missing from man's life. God decided that His communion with Adam, teaching Adam about Himself and His creation, was not fulfilling enough for Adam. Knowing how He made Adam, and the needs that He created him with, God purposed to make woman. It's very important to note that woman was created for man, from man. This fact explains why she is referred to as "the glory of the man." If you look at it correctly, that description is a great compliment; it places her in a place of high estimation.

In creating the woman, God looked at her as the one who could perfect His glory in the man. Her ministry to the man would enable him to be completely made in the image of God. Without the woman, the man will never reach his maximized potential in God.

Maximized Potential

There are three things a man needs in order to reach his maximized potential in God:

1. He needs the grace of God, which is the favor of God. Ephesians 2:8-9 says, "For by grace are ye saved through faith; and that not of yourselves: it is the gift of God: Not of works, lest any man should boast."

2. He needs the wisdom of God. Luke 2:52 says, ''And Jesus increased in wisdom and stature, and in favour with God and man.''

3. He needs the courage of God. Psalms 27:14 says, ''Wait on the Lord: be of good courage, and he shall strengthen thine heart....''

God created the woman so she could help the man move in the areas where he could obtain the grace, courage, and wisdom of God; she is to help him become all that God wants him to be.

<u>No Unisex</u>

God differentiates between the sexes. When God made Adam and Eve, He made them distinctly different; He did not make unisex. Neither did God make provision for homosexuality within the marriage covenant; He made them male and female. Men and women play distinctly different roles. We must not confuse or be offended by these roles, because God created us specifically as males and females.

I was in a church service where a woman jumped up and declared, ''We are all one in God!'' She was referring to Galatians 3:28, which says, ''There is neither Jew nor Greek, there is neither bond nor free, there is neither male nor female: for ye are all one in Christ Jesus.'' Her pastor attempted to reason with her by advising her that she was lifting the scripture out of its context. But she insisted that she was correct, saying, ''You are not any different from me.'' Finally, after all his attempts failed, the pastor made this statement: ''Well if you don't think there's any difference, you take your clothes off and I'll take mine off, and we'll see if there's a difference.''

I realize that was a rather drastic statement on his part, but when people are so insistent in their error, you have to be bold. There is no such thing as unisex. When we lift scriptures out of context, it leads to deception. People need not be confused about who is going to be the head and who will have the final say in the decision-making process; the roles are well-defined. And remember, the wife's role is not an inferior role, it's just different.

The Serpent

The serpent was a beautiful creature. One Hebrew expression says he was the zenith of God's creation. He was originally an upright creature, and he seemingly did something that none of the other animals could do. Although some theologians believe that the animal kingdom could at one time converse with Adam, we know for a fact (based on the scriptures) that this particular animal could talk. And it didn't seem to alarm Eve, either. In fact, she and the serpent seemed to communicate pretty well. But the serpent allowed Satan to enter into him; this resulted in the woman's deception. And the woman was deceived because she perceived or reasoned within her mind that the fruit was good to make one wise. Deception is always the result when you reason away the word of God.

After the Fall

And I will put enmity between thee and the woman, and between thy seed and her seed; it shall bruise thy head, and thou shalt bruise his heel.

*Unto the woman he said, I will greatly multiply
thy sorrow and thy conception; in sorrow thou
shalt bring forth children; and thy desire shall be
to thy husband, and he shall rule over thee.*

Genesis 3:15-16

God never intended for man to rule over the woman;
they were to rule and have dominion together. But after the
fall, when God spoke the words, "thy desire shall be to thy
husband," things changed. In this verse, the word desire
means "to overtake or master." So what God was actually
saying was, "You shall desire to master or overtake the man."
This spirit remains prevalent in many homes today.

The liberation movement has affected many women,
even within the body of Christ, about the role of men in
leadership. There are many talented, anointed women in the
church, but that is not enough. You can have the anointing of
God and still be out of order. Women must keep in mind who
they are. Miriam, the sister of Aaron and Moses, in murmuring
against Moses, became a testimony for seven days that you can
have the anointing of God but still be out of order. For not
honoring leadership, she paid a price and caused the entire
nation of Israel to suffer the consequences of her sin (Numbers
12:10-16).

We must beware because, in the days to come, a false
spirit shall come upon the church, pushing women to the
forefront. God uses women, but there is an order in how He
does it. When God called Moses, He called his family; when
God called me, He also called my wife. God would not call me
without calling my family (Many people have a problem with
family leadership, but that is how God operates at times). And
while God does use women, He will never place a woman in

a position of leadership over a man; that would violate His word.

God never violates His word. If you understand the scriptures, you should never sit up under a ministry that is headed by a woman. I don't have anything against women, but I understand order in the kingdom. God said, ''A bishop (the Greek word means pastor) then must be blameless, the husband of one wife...'' (1 Timothy 3:2). You cannot change the Scripture to say, ''... the wife of one husband...,'' and still be in agreement with God.

The terms ''desire and rule'' were never mentioned before the curse (Genesis 3:17). God never intended for a woman to be ruled; He never intended for a man to have to force a woman to do anything. These conditions came about after the fall, as a result of the curse. After the fall, the woman would not desire to be under subjection, but would attempt to overtake or master the man. This placed the man in a position to have to deny her or force her into subjection. This was not God's original plan.

It's wrong for a man to threaten his wife in order to get her to respond to him. In fact, if you use fear to get your wife to respond (attempting to manipulate her by withholding money, fellowship, clothing, food, bill payments, or your physical body and affections) you don't love her. And the unsubmissive wife doesn't really love her husband, either. The love of God in a woman's heart will cause her to willingly submit to her husband. She will understand that in submitting to the man, she is in effect submitting to God. In the same way, God's love in a man's heart will cause him to treat his wife with tenderness and love. Jesus never uses force--He appeals to us. I doubt the salvation of any man who beats his wife in order to get her to respond to his authority. He is less than a man!

God made it very plain that He would put enmity between the woman and the real culprit, Satan. Women, there is a very good reason why you should listen to your husbands. Something happened in the fall that you are not aware of, and most preachers today aren't proclaiming the truth about it. The word enmity in verse 15 means hostility. In that verse we learn that as a result of the fall, God allowed hostility to come between the woman and the devil, and between her seed and his seed. The verse is finished with these words: "... it [the woman's seed] shall bruise thy head, and thou shalt bruise his [the woman's seed] heel."

Through sin, women have been placed in a very vulnerable position. Satan's extreme hatred for women causes him to seek vengeance against them. It is through the covering of the man that the attacks of the enemy are rendered futile. When a woman submits to her husband, she comes under a divine covering or protection that is ordained of God; the enemy cannot penetrate this. So you can see, women, why it is so vital to your well-being to be in submission to your husbands.

Blessing or Cursing

Women, whether you know it or not, the devil hates you. The devil hates you more than he hates men because he knows that you have influence with the man. Satan knows that if he can cause the influence you have with your husband to become negative, your husband will never be able to accomplish anything.

Eve's influence in the life of Adam resulted in the fall. The serpent, Satan, used the woman to get to the covenant-keeper, Adam. Wives, your influence with your husbands can be for good; it does not have to be for evil. It depends on the choices you make. There are some husbands who will never be anything because their wives won't make the choice to help them become something. I am what I am today by the grace of God and because I have a good woman with me--my wife! (Notice that I said, ''my wife!'' It's important to remember that God is not the author of confusion. He will never call another woman to stand alongside a man; He will always call that man's wife).

Wives have the potential to bring their husbands into the place of blessing with God, or to cause them to be in opposition with God, causing the curse to fall upon them. Adam was the covenant-keeper, but there was a reason he listened to the voice of his wife. It's not because he should have (and I'm by no means trying to justify his actions), but there was a reason; he came under her influence.

In 1 Timothy 2:13-14, the Apostle Paul makes this statement: ''For Adam was first formed, then Eve. And Adam was not deceived, but the woman being deceived was in the transgression.'' Paul is saying that Eve was the one who was actually deceived. I'd like to make something very clear at this point: All sin is based upon unbelief, and unbelief is simply refusing to believe what God says. Sin is always entered into by an act of selfishness; it is always continued (or perpetuated) through a lie or deceit.

When we believe what God says in His word, then we must certainly know that sin will be punished. When we read the Bible and fail to do what it says, we become guilty of unbelief, just as Adam did. Adam and Eve were in the garden when the serpent came along and said, ''Yea, hath God said ...'' (Genesis 3:1). His words (the lie) began to work on Eve (the unbelief) and she began to reason within herself (the selfishness). God had said that partaking of the fruit (the act of disobedience) would cause death, and the seed of death was being planted.

God never intended for man to have a knowledge of evil. He never intended for you to be sick one day in your life. He never intended for you to know poverty, fear, calamity, or even death. Before the fall, Adam was in the kingdom of God and the kingdom was in him--the very life and nature of God was in Adam! Then came death.

Death is the absence of the life of God. Ephesians 2:1 says, "And you hath he quickened, who were dead in trespasses and sins...." When we're born-again we are made alive by the Spirit of God--we pass from death to life. Adam existed in a perfect environment and also held this perfection within himself. God had invested himself in Adam. Eve, on the other hand, received the commandment from Adam, not God. God dealt with Adam; Adam dealt with Eve. The devil understood this, and so he made his approach through Eve. So Adam gave God's command to Eve, but she rebelled. When she partook of the forbidden fruit, the glory of God disappeared; and when Adam looked on her, he saw that God's glory was gone. Then Adam made the fatal decision to also partake of the forbidden fruit. The Bible says that he was not deceived, but rather that he knew what he was doing, and that he loved the woman. In other words, Adam came under the woman's influence.

Eve used her influence with Adam for evil. Wives, you can either use your ministry to your husband, which is your influence with him, for good or evil. Let your decision be for good, which is according to the word of God.

Godly Fear and Humility

> *Submitting yourselves one to another in the fear of God.*
>
> Ephesians 5:21

Humble yourselves therefore under the mighty hand of God, that he may exalt you in due time.

1 Peter 5:6

The word "fear" in Ephesians is not referring to holy awe, but to terror. While this may seem strange to some, the Bible teaches that there is a difference. Proverbs 15:33 says, "The fear of the Lord is the instruction of wisdom." When you fear God and understand the price you will pay for walking contrary to His will, you are walking in the terror of the Lord. Now the Bible says that " ... perfect love casteth out fear ... " (1 John 4:18), but this is the type of fear that brings torment. It is done away with while the reverential fear remains.

The problem with most marriages today is that there is no fear or terror of God. Because submission in marriage is a divinely ordained principle, when you violate the submissive role in your family, you are actually involving God. And God has already gone on record as saying, "I'll take care of the guilty party" (Hebrews 10:30).

Because God ordained marriage, when a man and woman enter into the covenant of marriage, they not only enter into an agreement between themselves, they also enter into an agreement with God. It is this agreement with God that should cause married people to walk in the fear of God. God expects us to honor our part of the covenant; He is holding us responsible. So when you say, "I do," you'd better make sure you understand the fear of God. For while God is love (1 John 4:8), He is also known for His terror (2 Corinthians 5:11), and He will render justice.

Within the marriage covenant, there is a role of submission for both parties. It is just as important for a husband to submit to his wife, as it is for the wife to submit to her husband. In the body of Christ, there is no such thing as men who do not have to submit: There are no dictators, macho men, or rough-riding bronco-busters who are exempt from submitting. This is why humility is so vital to a successful marriage. You cannot properly submit to one another as God has directed you if you think too much of yourself. God will show you how to think about yourself; you don't have to overdo it.

"As unto the Lord"

Wives, submit yourselves unto your own hus-bands, as unto the Lord.

For the husband is the head of the wife, even as Christ is the head of the church: and he is the saviour of the body.

Therefore as the church is subject unto Christ, so let the wives be to their own husbands in every thing.

Ephesians 5:22-24

Submitting "as unto the Lord" does not mean that the wife is to obey her husband when it conflicts with what the Lord says. If the husband is obedient to God, then the wife is to submit to his authority.

There are men who have infiltrated the church and entrapped women. These men mimic tongues, praising God and dancing. They give the impression that they are of God when they actually have one foot in the church and the other in the world. When these men marry, they demand that their wives accompany them to and participate in all types of ungodly, worldly activities. They tell their wives, "The Bible says you're to be subject to me." They're misusing the word of God! A wife is not to follow her husband at this point. These type of men aren't saved, and women who follow them will end up backslidden. Women must make quality decisions if they want the God-kind of marriage.

In this passage from the book of Ephesians, God is really saying that the husband is the personal possession (or property) of the wife. Therefore, the wife can submit to him because he belongs to her. Wives, your husbands belong to you exclusively. Every inch of them belongs to you, from the crowns of their heads to the soles of their feet. God made them just for you.

A wife should never submit to her husband as though he were the Lord; there is only one Lord, and that is Jesus. The husband is the representative (or agent) of Jesus in the home and, as such, he functions in the role of the leader. As the husband follows Jesus, the wife can submit to him.

The book of Acts says " ... We ought to obey God rather than men" (5:29). There is a false teaching which states that the wife is supposed to go as far as her faith will take her: So that if her faith allows her to go to the bar, or the dance hall, or even to have an affair, that's what she should do. Nonsense! Drunkenness is drunkenness, adultery is adultery, and both are sin! God never sanctions sin. As long as your husband is following Christ, follow him; as long as he's speaking the word of God, submit to him. You're not to be in bondage to any man. John 8:36 declares, "If the Son therefore shall make you free, ye shall be free indeed."

Although there are many in our local assemblies who try to usurp (or steal) leadership's authority, there can only be one God-given leader; that's who you are to obey. It should be the same way in our homes. Whatever God is doing, He always shares it with the leader. Whether in the home or in the church, God always sends revelation knowledge through the leader. And it's not hard to obey when you realize that it's really God you're obeying, through man.

I've counseled many women who make the same mistake over and over. I've heard them say many times, ''He's not doing this... so I'm going to do it.'' What they've failed to keep in mind is that God never intended for the woman to take on the man's role. Because if the man ever starts walking right, he needs to walk in his own role and not have to contend with his wife. There can't be two heads in a marriage; anything with two heads is a freak! There can be only one leader; someone has to follow. So if your husband's not doing his part, don't take over his role; instead, turn things over into the hands of God. God will take care of you until your husband assumes his responsibility.

The Submission Principle

> *Wives, submit yourselves unto your own hus-bands [not another man--not your father, not your uncle, and not the preacher], as unto the Lord.*
>
> *For the husband [not the pastor, not the church, not an organization, not the doctrine, not your sister, and not your brother] is the head of the wife, even as Christ is the head of the church: and he is the saviour of the body.*
>
> Ephesians 5:22-23

There is a submission principle that must operate within a marriage. Submission means ''to subordinate, to reflect, to obey, to be under obedience, to put under or subdue, and to submit self unto.'' God wants both husband and wife to submit to His word.

Wives, when it comes to domestic relationships, you are to submit to one man, and that is your husband; you are his glory. The husband is to function as a sacrificial lover; he is to be everything that Jesus is. He is to lay down his life for his wife; he is to meet her every need; he is to take care of her spiritually, mentally, physically, and financially.

Following some teaching I'd done on domestic relationships, one of the women in my church asked me, ''Pastor, you've been teaching us all this truth and we're working at good jobs, but where are these men going to come from?'' What she really wanted to know was, were these men going to be on their level. I responded, ''They're going to have good jobs, too.'' Why would God establish the principle that everything reproduces after its own kind, make sure you're taught the truth so that you can properly develop in Him, and then send you a person who is way beneath your level? Why would God let you work, allowing you to accomplish something, and then send you a guy with no self-motivation and no discipline? God doesn't work like that!

The reason there is so much confusion about finding the proper mate is because people usually mishandle the situation. What generally happens when a woman meets a man is that she takes fire in her bosom because she allows him to hold, touch, and kiss her, arousing her passions. Then by the time she hears herself saying, ''I know it's wrong, but I love him. I know I shouldn't be caught up with him, but...,'' she's so emotionally involved that she can't turn away; so she starts believing the lie that ''God sent him.'' God has never and will never send a man of the flesh to a woman after the Spirit! This is an extremely negative situation and God will never sanction it. He never builds on a negative premise.

God will, however, initiate relationships. So in order not to miss the voice of God, singles must be consistent and watchful in prayer. Do not allow Satan to abort God's perfect will for your life.

The main reason so many marriages are dysfunctional is that most married couples are trying to straighten each other out. Instead of each person working on themselves, they inevitably end up pointing out and trying to improve the other person's faults. For example, so often when the relationship is not good, the husband will study Ephesians 5:22 and conclude that if his wife would just "submit" herself, everything would be alright. And the wife gets stuck on Ephesians 5:25: she knows everything would be fine if he'd just "love" her. The problem with that type of thinking, is that neither person is remembering their part; they're just thinking about what the other person should do. Yet each person's role is vital. As you apply Biblical principles to your marriage, you will begin to see your marriage become energized by the life of God that is in His word. You'll quit pointing fingers and start examining yourself. Revelation will come as you submit to God's word. You will find that you are able to submit to your spouse.

The Role of Submission

If you're going to have a happy marriage, you must understand the role and definition of submission. Submission involves a surrendering to authority. Yet in our modern day, people have a problem yielding to authority in every aspect of their lives. In our society, there is no respect for authority and this has carried over into the personal relationships between husbands and wives.

As I stated in an earlier chapter, the scriptures teach about "dual submission." Dual Submission is simply the husband submitting to his wife, and the wife submitting to her husband. Dual. Both ways. Yet most men, Christian men included, have a misguided concept of submission. Most men who occupy teaching positions within the church (pastors, preachers, teachers, etc...) pervert the principle of dual submission by only teaching one side of it: they put women under the feet of men. They operate as though they are ignorant of the scripture that says, "Submitting yourselves one to another ..." (Ephesians 5:21).

But since God has ordained that the principle of dual submission be operational in marriages, we must learn how to carry it out. The dual role of submission in marriage is directly related to the headship principle of the church: as the church submits to the Lord Jesus Christ, so the wife is to submit to the husband.

It's very simple; it's an issue of accountability. All authority in the earth has been delegated by God, and He has outlined everyone's position. When we understand that we are accountable to God because He has designed the program, and that He will judge all who violate His will, our problems with submission will disappear. Whether in our marriage, in the church, or on our jobs, we will find ourselves willing to submit.

Willing Submission

Jesus, as the head of the church, never forces the church to do anything. Jesus appeals to the church through the ministry of the Holy Spirit. The Holy Spirit bears witness; but if you don't act (or respond), He doesn't force you. This is the principle of willing submission: the Holy Spirit will lead only those who are willing to be led.

You can understand the ministry of the Holy Spirit better when you compare His methods with those that Satan employs. The Holy Spirit is ever gently requiring your willingess in order to move in your life. And the move of the Holy Spirit in your life always leaves His peace with you. Demons, on the other hand, will always drive and force you against your will. And yielding to demonic pressure always brings torment into your life.

As an under-shepherd of the Straight Gate Church, God has given me the mantle of apostolic impartation and divine authority. I dare not, however, force my pastoral authority upon the Straight Gate flock; I can only use my God-given authority on those who recognize it. God's not about forcing people. God knows He cannot force anyone to do anything pertaining to the kingdom of God. You must be willing.

Submission through Commitment

If ye love me, keep my commandments.

John 14:15

Jesus explains very clearly in this scripture that you demonstrate your love by (or through) your commitment. Two people should be in love when they marry, but they should not marry for love; they should marry for commitment.

The best way to put submission into operation in your marriage is through a commitment to one another. You will never be able to operate in God's divine submission by brow-beating your wife, or henpecking your husband; that is not God's way. But it is through your commitment to the Lord

Jesus Christ, as you make an appeal to Him to strengthen your marriage, you will begin to see the flow of God's divine submission into your marriage.

Because all truth is parallel, the amount of submission you furnish to God is the amount that will return to you in your human relationships, marriage included. If I, as a husband, do not have a good relationship with my wife, it's not her fault; the problem lies in my relationship with God. I need to ask myself, ''How fastened onto the things of God am I?''; ''Am I pursuing the Lord the way I should?'' Your relationship with God directly affects your relationship with your spouse. Develop a good relationship with God and watch your marriage flourish.

You demonstrate your love to God by your commitment to His word. My wife responds to me because of her commitment to God. I didn't write the law of the husband and wife--God did. If my wife loves God, she'll do what's right; if she doesn't love God, she won't. But if she fails to do what's right, I know what to do: I'm going to make an appeal to God, because He can speak to her. God can even wake my wife up in the middle of the night and talk to her. He knows what to do!

If you are a wife who is not being submissive to her husband, you are also not being submissive to the Lord. Because the Lord has set up delegated authority, it is impossible for you to submit to Him without submitting to your husband; the two go hand in hand. And if your husband slips up and does something wrong, don't base your reaction on his wrong action. The devil is a master at getting people to respond to wrong actions with wrong actions; but that's not God's way. You can live above that when you operate in the principle of submission. Because even when your spouse is wrong, you will still be able to submit because you understand that you're really submitting to the Lord. This type of thinking will revolutionize your marriage; that's why the devil fights it so hard. Your attitudes and actions are to be the result of your commitment and obedience to the things of God. This is the center (or heart) of your marriage.

Submission through Love

> *Wives, submit yourselves unto your own husbands, as it is fit in the Lord.*
>
> *Husbands, love your wives....*
>
> Colossians 3:18-19

The word "submit" in verse 18 is the same term used in Ephesians 5:21. The Greek definition means "to line up or to come up underneath." In other words, you fall in line with what God has said. That is all submission entails. Paul is speaking to the wives, saying, "You come up underneath and fall in line with your husbands."

What the majority of women fear most about submitting to their husbands is that he will misuse or abuse his position. And so often women do find themselves in situations that cause them to think thoughts like these: "This guy that I'm supposed to submit to is a tyrant! He acts like a monarch or a dictator! He rules with a rod of iron! He acts like he's the king, but I'm not his queen. In fact, he treats me like I'm his slave! He never has any good or warm words to say to me; I can't respond to him." I am grieved that women would have to be in a situation that causes them to think like this. Submission should not be achieved through oppression. God's way is to draw women into submission through love.

The wife will respond to the love of her husband just as the church of God responds to the love of our Lord Jesus. The ability of the church to submit to Jesus is predicated upon His love for us. In the same way, the wife's submission to her husband is based upon his love for her. The husband should function to the wife in the same role that Christ functions to the church--that of the sacrificial lover. This requires a demonstrative type of love. Now I realize that many men don't know how to demonstrate this Christ-like love; they lack the training. But that's okay, because now that you have the Holy Ghost, He will teach you! As He releases the wisdom of God into your lives, you will find the most beautiful creature on the face of the earth--your wife!--coming up underneath you, and falling in line with you. Your love for her will draw her into submission to you. You will find that you can have God's ideal marriage right here on earth. You can change things around!

Reverence Your Husband

> *Nevertheless let every one of you in particular so love his wife even as himself; and the wife see that she reverence her husband.*

> Ephesians 5:33

As found in Strong's Exhaustive Concordance, the Greek word for "reverence" is phobeo. This means that the wife is to have a type of reverential fear for her husband. According to the Greek definition, she is to revere him or respect him through an awe or reverential fear of him. The Amplified Bible explains it this way in 1 Peter 3:2:

> *When they observe the pure and modest way in which you conduct yourselves, together with your*

reverence [for your husband. That is, you are to feel for him all that reverence includes]--to respect, defer to, revere him; [revere means] to honor, esteem [appreciate, prize]; and (in the human sense) adore him; [and adore means] to admire, praise, be devoted to, deeply love and enjoy [your husband].

Wives, your husband belongs to you. By standing in awe of him and displaying reverence and respect for him, you will build him up and strengthen him. Speak words of life to him: tell him he's a good father; tell him you appreciate him; tell him you love him for going out and working for the family. If he messes up, and sometimes he will, tell him good things anyway. Then get on your face and cover him in prayer. Cook his meals; keep his house clean; keep yourself looking good for him. As you reverence your husband in this way, new life will come into your marriage. And you will experience the joy of walking in the reality of Galatians 6:5: "... whatsoever a man soweth, that shall he also reap."

The reason why so many people do not have happy marriages is because the wives think all they have to do is pray. And while prayer is important, prayer alone is not enough. The wife must learn to esteem, praise, and admire her husband, as well as pray for him. God created the man to respond to the admiration of a woman; and not only does the man like it, he needs it! If you're asking yourself why doesn't God take care of those needs in a man, you must remember that God created the woman to minister to the man. Why should God do your job?

Now, a woman should be spending time in prayer for her husband so that God can draw him closer, giving him a greater thirst and desire to walk in the things of God. Sisters, your ministry should never be for yourselves; you were not created to operate for yourself. You were created to be a help meet for a man, to help him do what God has called him to do. You were not called to establish your own ministry. Because women have a greater opportunity to work inside of the home, while men usually work outside of the home, they usually have more time to get involved in the things of God. But what often happens in these cases is the women make the mistake of studying for their own purposes.

Some years back, a guest speaker visited our church. At the last minute, she had to cancel because her husband experienced a heart attack. When I called her two days later to inquire about her husband's health, she said to me, "Yes, he had a heart attack because he didn't obey God-- he wouldn't help me in my ministry. But now he's going to submit and help me...." I was saddened by her reply. God doesn't give people heart attacks. And more importantly, God was not trying to get her husband to support her ministry. She was supposed to be his help meet, not the other way around. And people are still confused about this issue. It's important to learn what the word of God says so that you won't be operating in error.

A Meek and Quiet Spirit

...While they behold your chaste conversation coupled with fear.

Whose adorning let it not be that outward adorning of plaiting the hair, and of wearing of gold, or of putting on of apparel;

But let it be the hidden man of the heart, in that which is not corruptible, even the ornament of a meek and quiet spirit, which is in the sight of God of great price.

1 Peter 3:2-4

It is very important for women to understand how God feels about a meek and quiet spirit: God will not look at you as a woman of God if you do not possess this quality. You will never get to the throne room of God with a haughty spirit: ''God resisteth the proud, but giveth grace unto the humble'' (James 4:6). So you can see how necessary it is to your salvation to understand what a meek and quiet spirit is, and to make sure you are clothed in it.

The word ''quiet'' in the Greek means ''silent.'' There's a saying in the world: Silence is golden. But when you understand that saying in the context of the Scriptures, you realize how true it is. Let's take for example arguing. How many times have you found yourself persisting in an argument because you wanted to get the last word in? It's not so unusual; in fact, it's typical worldly behavior. But it's not God's way.

The more I see of God and the more I understand the Scriptures, the more I see how often we violate them. Husbands, you can't curse your wives and then pray. You see, God refuses to hear a man who won't take care of his house. I'm not just referring to putting bread on the table; I mean functioning in a godly manner. And, on the other hand, if a woman has a spirit that's not submissive to her husband, God's not going to honor her prayers either. God doesn't tell the wife to be submissive and then listen to her prayers if she's haughty. You can pray all night, or even for the rest of your life, but God won't hear you!

Let's read 1 Peter 3:3-4 again: ''Whose adorning let it not be that outward adorning of plaiting the hair, and of wearing of gold, or of putting on of apparel; But let it be the hidden man of the heart ....'' God wants His women to be properly adorned. Women of God should not be adorned only on the outside because it is the inward adorning that wins the godly man. But Peter isn't saying that you shouldn't wear nice clothes and fine jewelry or fix your hair up. He's simply saying that you won't win a godly husband with purely natural things.

God made men to appreciate the way women look; an attractive woman appeals to a man. Because God set it up this way, He wants women to look their best. Take my wife for example: she knows how I like her to dress. I take her to the store and I help her pick out her clothes, because she's dressing for me. She understands this and she's not offended by my involvement. And if she bought a dress that I didn't like, she'd willingly take it back because she wants to please me.

I want my wife to look well-cared for; I don't want her to look out of style. So in addition to providing clothing for her, I support her trips to the hairdresser. I encourage her to do whatever she needs to do to look good. This type of attention pleases my wife and makes her more responsive to me. She knows she's dressing for me, and no other man. No one else is involved--just her and me. It's a wonderful part of the husband-wife relationship. Women thrive under the care and attention of their husbands; God made them that way. So I always encourage the husbands to make those shopping trips that they really don't enjoy going on. (But I also tell the women to use wisdom and not keep them there too long!)

But remember, women (and men!) can go to the extreme on the outward appearance. So if you don't have a meek and a quiet spirit to help you submit to the things of God, you're asking for trouble.

I'd like to touch some more on wives dressing for their husbands. You are married to one man, and he's the man you should be seeking to please. When you shop or fix your hair, in everything you do to look your best, your mind should be on your husband and what he likes. Wives should not be seeking compliments from other men. This means that if your husband doesn't like your hairstyle, you do something about it.

Now I'm aware that a man doesn't always know what hairstyle looks best on a woman, so you may have to educate your husband. You can buy a book and show him some styles; give him some options to choose from. You should be glad your husband is taking an interest in you, so do whatever you can to help him along; in doing so, you'll be helping yourself.

"Calling Him Lord"

> *For after this manner in the old time the holy women also, who trusted in God, adorned themselves, being in subjection unto their own husbands. Even as Sarah obeyed Abraham, calling him lord....*
>
> 1 Peter 3:5

I used to tell my wife to call me "lord." I know that sounds a bit extreme, and actually it probably was, but I was really attempting to make a point: I was trying to teach Vickey the principle behind Sarah's calling Abraham lord. In the Greek, "lord" means provider and protector. Because I'm my wife's provider and protector, her covering, I'm her lord. Now that doesn't mean wives have to call their husbands lord, but it is important to understand the principle of the man's lordship as appointed to him by God. The "lord" of a household--the man, the husband, the father--is the God-appointed protector and provider for all who come under his authority. It is a high position to occupy and one that carries a great burden of responsibility. The wife is relieved of this burden because God gave it to the man. That is why submission is so important. The lordship principle can only operate the way it should when the wife has a meek and quiet spirit. God has tied His principles together in such a way that in order for one to work properly, another one has to be obeyed.

God-Appointed Positions

When the husband goes off to work, in his God-appointed position as provider for his family, the wife should be operating in her God-appointed position as caretaker within the home. Now I realize that in this day and age it's not always possible for the wife to stay within the home, but that does not change the fact that it is God's appointed position for her. I would advise every Godly woman to seek the Lord and do all she can to move into her God-designed role as caretaker in the home; it is God's way and it is the best way. It may mean getting along with less money, but the tradeoff is well worth it. You don't need as much money as you think to make your husband feel special and to take good care of your children, and the home just functions better when the wife is in it.

She is able to move in her role as an intercessor, covering her husband (and her children) with her prayers. Because the workplace (and, sadly, even the schools) are filled with such violence, with unsaved men and women practicing all types of vices, intercession by the wife and mother is essential. The idea of a wife sitting home idly all day long, watching TV and eating chocolates, has no place in the life of a godly woman; there's no time for it! Satan is busy and we need to be alert and watching in prayer.

The Heart of the Home

The wife is the heart of the home. That's why the devil tries so hard to discredit her. One way in which the enemy makes his attack against women is through the medium of TV--television is filled with programs that exploit women. The woman is the heart of the home and Satan desperately wants to undermine her ability to exert a godly influence in the home. If the devil can discredit her, he will be successful in his attempts to bring confusion into the home. The Bible speaks of "confusion and every evil work" going hand in hand (James 3:16). This is Satan's strategy. But he cannot do it when the wife is watching in prayer, covering her husband so that he can move in his role as the leader of the family. Stand your ground! Don't allow the devil to move in your homes!

Chapter Eight

The Winning Lifestyle

Likewise ye wives, be in subjection to your own husbands; that if any obey not the word, they also may without the word be won by the conversation [the lifestyle] of the wives.

1 Peter 3:1

There are many women who love God with all of their heart, soul, mind, and strength, but who have husbands that are not saved. These wives are actively seeking God on their husband's behalf, claiming their salvation by faith; but for the present time, these men are not saved.

Now I'd like to speak a word of direction into the lives of these wives: you will never get your husband to obey the Word of God by leaving tracks under his pillow, badgering him about coming to church, or threatening him with going to hell. You will not get him saved any other way than by doing what the Bible says in 1 Peter 3:1 : ''... they also may without the word be won by the conversation [or conduct] of the wives.'' Men are to be won to Christ by the daily walk (lifestyle) of their wives. Witnessing is more than verbal expression. Your ''conversation'' is your lifestyle; it must be your witness.

You've no doubt heard that old cliche, ''Actions speak louder than words.'' It's like a woman who comes to church, gets filled with the Holy Ghost, professes to love God, gets a big Bible to study, but has the dirtiest house on the block. When her husband comes home, she's never there. Where is she? She's in some meeting casting out demons. Her husband's clothes are not clean, there's no food on the table, and the children are being neglected because she's become the ''Annie Oakley'' of the Christian Church. This is not the way to win your husband to Christ. God's way is for the man to ''behold your chaste conversation coupled with fear [godly reverence]....''

You will never get your husband, or anyone else for that matter, saved by talking on the telephone all the time. The longer you talk, the greater the temptation becomes to discuss things that you shouldn't. There's little use in telling your husband to get saved after he has heard you run down the pastor and everyone else in the church. The next time you try to convince him to go to church, he will look at you and say something similar to this: ''Hey! If you're like this, all the rest of them must be like this!'' He doesn't know that you're the exception to God's standard. If he came to church he'd see that many of the people truly represent Christ. Wives, when you don't line up with the Word of God, you are really interfering with your husband's salvation.

Many women have husbands who are not Spirit-filled. They are not functioning as sacrificial lovers. They're not giving spiritual, mental, emotional, or financial support. In essence, these types of husbands are really doing harm to the home. So the wife may ask, "How do I get this man to turn around?" Well, you don't get him to turn around by telling everyone in the congregation what he's not doing; and asking everyone to pray for him won't do it either. You get him to turn around by your winning lifestyle.

Another thing the Scriptures do not teach is for wives to constantly badger their husbands with the pastor's words. When you say, "The pastor said this and the pastor said that..." you really turn your husband off; he doesn't want to hear what the pastor says. Don't attempt to use the pastor to whip your husband into shape. The Bible plainly says that if you have a husband that doesn't obey the Word,"...they may also without the word be won...." But again, that winning occurs through the wife's lifestyle, not her nagging.

Wives, your lifestyle and conversation, along with your demonstration of purity, consecration, dedication, and commitment to God will win your husband to the Lord. You don't need tracts; you don't need to play Gospel music all day; you don't need to get out of your bed at night and pray to the extent that he can't sleep; and you certainly don't need to turn your house into a prayer meeting or Bible study location. But by your lifestyle, consecration, and dedication, as a godly woman, you'll win him.

The Woman's Ministry

A wife's first ministry is in her home, to her husband, her family. There has been a great deal of teaching on this, but we're still doing everything except for what God has told us to do. The ministry that God has laid out for women can be found in Titus 2:4-5:

That they may teach the young women to be sober,

to love their husbands, to love their children,

To be discreet, chaste, keepers at home, good, obedient to their own husbands, that the word of God be not blasphemed.

There are too many women in the church today who are running around trying to minister in the things of God, while neglecting the ministry in their homes. God gives the home ministry top priority; He has ordained it to be the woman's first ministry. This doesn't mean women can't have a ministry outside of the home. God only requires that "all things be done decently and in order" (1 Corinthians 14:40). Your first ministry after God is in your home. If you're married, your first ministry is to your husband.

Yet we're living in a society in which exploitation, the breakdown of the family unit, and the demise of societal standards are prevalent. While these circumstances should force us to renew our minds, we instead see a carry-over of the world's standards into the church; this in turn affects the family unit. It is very difficult for a woman to learn how to minister to a man if she is a product of the world's thinking concerning men.

We must remember that the church makes up the only normal people in the world. Everyone else in the world is perverted or abnormal because they have decided to live without the standards of God. Look at the type of women the world exalts: Hollywood's standard is not for the church! Yet, sadly, there are women in the church who want to be just like the ungodly, worldly women that are set before them. We should not look to the world for our standards.

When the holiness/pentecostal movement came along, it did some good; but in another sense, it also did some bad.

They were right when they taught separation; we are to be separate from the world. But they were wrong when they taught isolation. We cannot make an impact unless there is contact. The world has to see that there is a difference between them and the church.

The Wise Home-Builder

> *Every wise woman buildeth her house: but the foolish plucketh it down with her hands.*

> Proverbs 14:1

Building relationships is of primary importance to God. Outside of your relationship with Him, God is most concerned about who you're going to spend the rest of your life with. Jesus is your first priority; your spouse comes next. So by faith, you need to see your spouse whole in every area of their life.

Through the word of God, the wise woman is constantly building on her foundation, brick by brick. This process is a slow, laborious one, and we can probably understand it better by looking at it in the natural. If you were going to build your home, you couldn't do it in a day, a week, or possibly even in a year. Bit by bit you would put it together, but the first thing you would do is make sure you had a solid foundation. If the foundation has been placed improperly, it is inevitable that problems will develop in the future. And so it is with the building of our spiritual homes.

When trouble develops in a marriage, a wise woman will realize that she has been doing something wrong. So just like in the natural, she will go and rent a bulldozer, uproot everything that she's built incorrectly, take good bricks and resume building from there. The problem that seems to occur with most women is that they are constantly building on the wrong foundation; any foundation other than the word of God must be uprooted. When you didn't have godly knowledge you thought like the world. But the world doesn't know how a man thinks, how God made a man to be, or what he requires from a woman. This is why it is so necessary for the people of God to have their minds washed with the word of God--the old must be washed away and replaced by the new.

God made women with a mystique. This is good, it is what attracts men to women. The clothes, the smell, the subtleness--all of these things appeal to men. But feminine mystique alone is not enough to keep a relationship going. The world operates in feminine mystique and their relationships fail all the time. There is something more that God requires.

God has established the principle of women reverenc-ing their husbands. The best marriages are built upon this principle. A woman who operates in this principle will have a profound effect on her husband; her admiration and esteem for him will greatly enhance their relationship. She'll dem-onstrate her feelings toward him by meeting him at the door when he comes home from work. When they're out with other couples, she'll boast about her husband; the theme of her conversation will be her husband, and he'll just soak it up.

Now, she's not lying or falsely representing either herself or her husband; she's speaking from the genuineness of her heart, her true feelings for her husband. She's come to the place where she understands that in order for her husband to function in her life the way she needs him to, he must feel her admiration, sense her reverence. So she actively displays it. When he comes home tired and the children are noisy, she'll instruct them to keep quiet while their father sleeps. She'll often remind him, "I'm so glad you chose me... I'm so glad

I'm your wife. I appreciate you going out and working, providing for me and the children, providing our home and meeting our needs ...." There are not too many rationally thinking men that can resist this type of treatment.

Yet I'm well aware that there are many husbands who don't deserve this type of treatment; based on their actions and behavior they haven't earned the right to any of this good treatment. But let's move beyond the appearance of things and try to deal with this on a spiritual level. If you're wondering if you should still apply the principle of reverence even when your husband doesn't apparently deserve it, the answer is a resounding "YES!" Why? The Bible declares in Proverbs 18:21, "Death and life are in the power of the tongue ...." Women, you have the ability to speak life into your husbands' lives, into your marriages. Your words have power. Proverbs 6:2 says, "Thou art snared with the words of thy mouth, thou are taken with the words of thy mouth." So take your apparent unpleasant circumstances and use them as opportunities to plant seeds of life into your husband's life. If your husband is not bringing any income home, you want to change his image of himself (the enemy is already trying to beat his self-image down; you want to counteract that). So you'll want to say things like, "You're the best provider; I appreciate you...Is there anything I can do to make it better and easier for you? ... I enjoy running your bath water, washing your clothes ...." These are words of life; they will elevate him and encourage him to do better.

This reminds me of a woman, a sister in the church, who complained and complained, bad mouthing her husband to the pastor, until she finally convinced him to come to their home and speak with her husband. As the three of them sat in this sister's home, she released a barrage of complaints against her husband, venting every displeasing thing she could think of. Her husband just sat there and watched her; he was embarrassed that she was telling another man about his faults. (I'd like to pass along a bit of advice at this point: men do not like to be compared to other men, even the pastor. For the most part, they don't even want to hear about the pastor. So women, a word to the wise--learn to relate to your husband, and leave the pastor out.) When this sister finally finished spewing out her venom (and you must remember that words can kill), her husband turned to the pastor and said, "I've listened to everything that she's said, and some of it is true; but I'll tell you why I do the things that she's accused me of. She's not a clean woman--she doesn't keep herself or our home clean. When I come home, there's rarely a home-cooked meal, and she doesn't say hello. She's not a good wife mentally, physically, or in any other way." This sister was so embarrassed she almost fainted. But the truth was, she was actually destroying her home because she was not building on godly principles. Instead of pointing a finger at her husband, she should have gone back, re-examined her foundation, pulled up what was bad, and started building it again.

The wise woman builds her house; cleaning, cooking, and caring for her husband is part of that process. (Now don't get mad at me. I know it's the 1990's, but God's way is still right; and it still works!) It's very important that the wife understand the difference between her ministry to her husband and her ministry to her children. You are to love your children, but you are never to transfer your love for your husband to your children. You are to love them, but there is a special love you should have for your husband. After all, you are joined as one to your husband (Genesis 2:24), not to your children. You must never put your children in the place of your husband, or before your husband, by catering to their preferences and neglecting his; you will bring trouble into your marriage this way.

Wives are to make their husbands feel special. This requires some calculated efforts on your part, women. You're going to have to pray and ask God to show you how to make your husband feel special. If your husband doesn't know how to dress, take a subtle approach. Try telling him, ''Honey, I love you so much. I've saved up a few dollars and I'd like to take you shopping.'' Then help him pick out the clothes that make him look his best. Take time with him, giving him your opinion and advice. By making your husband feel special, you'll become special to him.

Sometimes women complain about not being special to their husbands, about not being able to keep their husbands at home. Take a few moments to honestly examine yourself and your situation. It's very possible that you're not doing what it takes to be interesting to him. When God made woman, He made her with a certain mystique. There should be a certain mystery about a woman which makes it necessary for a man to discover what's in her. In order to keep a man's interest, women must learn how to retain this air of mystery, even within the marital relationship.

Women can remain mysterious by their conduct. The way a woman calls her husband's name, the little pet names she uses with him, can draw him to her. The way she looks in his eyes, the unspoken feelings that pass between them, will keep him interested in her. The way she serves his food, taking such care and interest in all the little things that make up a meal, will provoke his thinking toward her. The way she keeps her house, so welcoming and inviting, will cause him to relax in her presence and let his guard down. He'll want to draw near to her, to uncover who she is, to discover this woman that makes him feel so good. And women, you can set the mood in your bedrooms for the way you want things to go. In the book of the Song of Solomon you'll find guidelines for keeping your bedroom. It's a very special room and you should keep it accordingly. It shouldn't be the junkiest room in the house and it shouldn't be a playroom for the children (neither should they sleep in your bed; the marital bed is for the husband and wife). Try buying some satin sheets and perfume and practice what the word of God says. Get rid of the worldly thinking that has been programmed into you.

Pray and Get Out of the Way

One of the godly woman's most powerful weapons is prayer; it can move mountains in her life. As you begin to operate within the principle of prayer, you will find your actions and reactions changing. Where you felt before that you just had to take action, you just had to do something, with prayer you'll find that you are able to wait on the Lord to move (and His action brings much better results than ours).

One area in which women must learn to "pray and get out of the way" is in the area of running the home. Now I know that some of you have husbands who are less than reliable; you just know he'll mess it up if you leave it to him. But you need to take another approach and look at your situation through the eyes of God. Lay the groundwork in prayer. Encourage him by your words--speak life into your situation! Then watch the hand of God move in your lives.

One mistake that the sisters have been making is that they've been unknowingly working against themselves. How? By the destructive words they've allowed the enemy to trick them into speaking against their husbands. So many of you keep saying what your husband is not; you need to change your confession and speak what he can become. Look your husband in the eyes and tell him, "I'm so glad you're my husband. I know you've done your best; I think you're the best provider in the world.'' Then use your influence to lead him into godly principles--not through preaching, but through your lifestyle. You'll see the hand of God move in your life in a way that you could not imagine. That man that you knew was not any good, will become, under your godly influence, the best possible mate. And all because you made the quality decision to pray and get out of the way.

Husband Ministry

> *The aged women likewise...*
>
> *That they may teach the young women to be sober, to love their husbands, to love their children,*
>
> *To be discreet, chaste, keepers at home, good, obedient to their own husbands....*
>
> Titus 2:3-5

Most women have not been taught how to minister to men. Where do you suppose this learning process was to come from? It was to come from the aged or mature women in the church. God never intended for the pastor to be in that role. My role as pastor of the Straight Gate Church is to seek the mind of God and minister what thus saith the Lord. The women in the Straight Gate Church can talk with my wife, or any of the other women that we recommend (there are some women in the church that we don't want the young women to speak with; we don't want these young sisters to be given the wrong advice) when they are in need of domestic and sexual relations counseling. If you talk to the wrong person about problems you are experiencing in your marriage, you will increase your problems. It's no one's business but yours what goes on in your house. The best thing any woman with marital problems can do is learn to talk to Jesus about them. He will show you how to be a godly help meet, thus solving many of your problems.

When you begin to get into the word of God, praying and studying the things of God, you'll discover what a wonderful Counselor He is. Someone once said, ''You can talk to Him anytime you need Him; even if you call Him up in the midnight hour, He's there.'' This is what having a relationship with God is all about--you know He'll be there when you need Him. A lot of the problems that people, particularly women, are having today in the body of Christ, are related to our leaning on the arm of flesh instead of the arm of God. Jesus never intended for us to know Him through men; that's why He gave us the Holy Spirit (John 16:13; 1 John 2:27). And once women become aware of what their true relationship with God can and should be, they begin to change.

The time you used to spend badgering your husband to do something, you'll now spend praying for God to draw him near. You'll find yourself on your face, praising God and praying that God will mold your husband by moving in his life; you'll pray God's favor upon him. This is true husband ministry. The Scriptures say, in John 6:44, ''No man can come to me except the Father which hath sent me draw him: and I will raise him up at the last day.'' Wives, you are the instrument, the tool, that Almighty God will use to draw your husband to Him. Don't take this lightly; don't allow Satan to deceive you. Stop wasting your time beating at the air and shadow boxing. Learn how to fight according to Ephesians 6:12: ''For we wrestle not against flesh and blood, but against principalities, against powers, against the rulers of the darkness of this world, against spiritual wickedness in high places.'' Now move into your ministry and tear the devil's kingdom down!

Chapter Nine

Delegated Authority

But I would have you know, that the head of every man is Christ; and the head of the woman is the man; and the head of Christ is God.

1 Corinthians 11:3

Delegated authority operates in this order: the Godhead (Father, Son, and Holy Spirit); the husband (in the domestic relationship); the wife. All authority in the earth is delegated authority. It comes from God, who has the ultimate authority; He delegates authority.

In the domestic relationship, there is not just a submitting to the man; there's a submitting also to the woman. Most men (preachers included) misinterpret the Scriptures on submission. To many people, submission is woven around a false concept of the husband's preferential position. This false submission is played out through the seating arrangements in many churches. These men sit on the front rows, by themselves, while their wives struggle in the back of the churches, trying to keep their children in order. This type of thinking has no place in the body of Christ. If you're going to be God's man and move in the husband's role, you must learn to be your wife's lover, and not a dictator.

There are Scriptures in the Bible that speak directly to the husband. The man is responsible for reading those Scriptures and examining himself. God never intended for the husband to burden his wife by saying, "You'd better do what I say." God never intended for the man to compare his wife to what the word says she should do. Although you may find that your wife has a tiny splinter in her eye, chances are that you'll find a great, big log in yours. Men, the authority in the home has been delegated to you by Jesus Christ; but you also have a head to submit to. You are not released to function in your marriage like some hot-shot dictator.

When Jesus says that the head of every woman is the man, He is talking about her husband. Some preachers incorrectly teach that within a particular church, every woman is subject to every man; that is not godly doctrine. Don't try to tell another man's wife what to do, and don't let any man violate your covenant with your wife by allowing him to tell her what to do. You have one wife; that's who you are responsible for. She is to be subject to you, and you only. This is delegated authority. This is the man's headship role.

Headship Misconceptions

One of the main misconceptions of headship is that the head is one who snaps a bullwhip and makes constant demands. Many men want a master-slave relationship with their wives; this is totally unscriptural. This type of thinking shows up in different ways. I used to associate with a brother who had a large, formal dining room in his beautiful, spacious home.

In the dining room, he had a big table with many chairs around it. At the head of the table he had a large chair, specially made. No one, including his wife, sat in that chair because it indicated that he was king. It was apparent that this man thought he was better than his wife. If you think like this, your wife will sense it, and it will cause a division between you.

The second misconception is seeing headship as equivalent to perfection. Some men believe they can walk on water. I call this man Mr. Waterwalker. A man like this thinks it is his job to have everything under his complete control at all times. Now, we all know that we're not God, we're not perfect. Yet this type of man looks for absolute perfection which is based upon the philosophy that "I really have it all together. I look good; I smell good; I have better sense than anyone else. I can do anything!" If you have a husband who is a Mr. Waterwalker, you will have to learn to live as his wife, continuing to pray, until God changes that man.

The third misconception is the "I am the head" syndrome. This poor guy is sure that his headship means he is to issue ongoing proclamations about the position God has given him. From the time he walks in the door his proclamations start. "The king is home!", he says with a loud voice (his family's probably thinking "Oh, no!" at this point). "I am the head!", he continues to exclaim (as if he ever let them forget!). All of this man's conversation includes the fact that spiritually he is the head. He constantly reminds his wife and children of this fact, saying "I'm the head of this family; you do what I say. You don't make any decisions around here, because I'm the head." His whole concept is this "I am the head" syndrome; he can't see anything else. He tells his wife (and this is really bad for a marriage), "God made me the head; don't talk--I'm the head!" Even when his wife gently asks, "Dear, couldn't we talk about it?", he still can't break out of his mold. ''What's there to talk about?'', he asks; ''the head has made the decision.'' This type of man is walking in ignorance, and he will alienate his wife from himself; women don't do well with this type of treatment. In order for him to understand what the Holy Spirit would like to show him, he must examine the Scriptures.

Family Headship

> *For the husband is the head of the wife, even as Christ is the head of the church: and he is the saviour of the body.*
>
> *Therefore as the church is subject unto Christ, so let the wives be to their own husbands in every thing.*
>
> *Husbands, love your wives, even as Christ also loved the church, and gave himself for it;*
>
> *That he might sanctify and cleanse it with the washing of water by the word.*
>
> Ephesians 5:23-26

Family headship involves the husband first receiving delegated authority from God, and then being held accountable by God for how he handles it.

Headship is not domination; it is not a hierarchy where the husband rules through fear and force. When I say that the man is the high priest or the head of his home, this means that he is the leader. And because he occupies this position of authority, God holds him responsible for the marriage. The woman, on the other hand, is an heir of God and a joint-heir with Jesus, just like the man (Romans 8:17). But her role is different. She is to submit to the man's leadership. So husbands should rule or lead through love, sensitivity, kindness, and warmth. In other words, a husband should lead his wife in such a manner that she'll want to do what he says--she'll want to submit. He won't achieve this by acting like some mad tyrant. He will achieve it by a demonstration of love.

So while the first part or responsibility of family headship is for the husband to keep order in the home, the second part is for him to love his wife as Christ loved the church (Ephesians 5:25). His role is to rule or minister to his wife in love--he is to function as her sacrificial lover.

Sacrificial Love

Men within the body of Christ must learn how to be sacrificial lovers. Husbands (and even grooms-to-be and single men) must learn the principle of sacrificial love. Christ loved the church so very much, that He gave Himself for it. The church has needs. There are people within it who are weak, sick, and burdened with problems. As these people go to the Head of the church (Jesus Christ), He responds out of love by meeting their needs. Your attitude towards your wife should always be one where you are willing to sacrifice for the purpose of meeting her needs; her needs come first, yours second. Christ is our example and we must look to Him to show us the way. Luke 11:9-10 assures us of what the response of Christ will be when we turn to Him with our needs: "And I say unto you, Ask, and it shall be given you; seek, and ye shall find; knock, and it shall be opened unto you. For every one that asketh receiveth; and he that seeketh findeth; and to him that knocketh it shall be opened." There's no doubt about it. If you come to Jesus, the Head of the church, and present your need, He will meet it! And God is saying to the husbands, ''In the same way that Christ loves His church and faithfully meets their needs, you are to become the sacrificial lovers in your homes, faithfully meeting the needs of your wives.''

Through sacrificial love, the man is to cause the woman to come under subjection to him, drawing her to him in love. The husband, as the head, is responsible for the relationship. He is to cause his wife to come under subjection through his display of love, kindness, consideration, appreciation, protection, provision, and preservation towards her. God created women to respond to sacrificial love by willingly submitting to their husbands.

God is a spirit. He is also love, and He expresses His love through words. Yet God went beyond words by creating the human family to express Himself in the earth. This is why God regards the marital relationship so highly and takes such an interest in the success of it. The Bible says that the woman was created to help the man. Yet some men feel they are so strong, smart, and determined that they can do everything by themselves. Adam was created with a lack; the woman was made to complete that lack. In order to have the God-kind of marriage, a man must not exclude his wife. A man should never say he can make it on his own. However far you feel you can get by yourself, you will be ten miles further down the road with your wife at your side.

Sacrificial love is demonstrated love. In the same way that God demonstrated His love for us by giving His Son for us while we were yet sinners (Romans 5:8), husbands are to love their wives. She should not have to earn it; it should pour from you.

The Meaning of Love

Love can mean many things. A woman may ''love''

her hairstyle or her outfit; a boy may "love" hamburgers; some men "love" sports; many people "love" their pets. When love is used in these ways, what does it mean? Does it mean you would give your all for clothes, food, sports, or a pet? Probably not. Does it mean you would sacrifice everything for a hamburger? Of course not. Or that you would put the well-being of your pet above everything else in your life? No, that's not what this type of love means. In fact, it's really not love; it's really a liking or a preference for something. It can even be warm feelings for something, like your pet, but it's not really love. Love is different; it's higher, it's from God. Let's look at love from God's point of view. We'll use Greek terminology to help us see the different shades of meaning of the word love.

The first type of love is Stoic love. This type of love is used to describe the love of animals. It also describes the love between members of a family, like a parent and a child (husbands and wives do not love each other with Stoic love).

The next type of love is Eros. Eros is erotic love. It is based on sexual desire and does not necessarily involve any form of commitment or responsibility. The world pushes this type of love. You see it in operation through the sexual exploitation of women in the media. Advertisements are full of women being used in an attempt to physically arouse men so they will buy a car or some other item. Women are constantly shown being exploited in TV programs and movies. And the thing about it is, it works! There is that part in man (and woman!) that responds to the Eros type of love. That in itself is not bad; it is the way it is handled apart from God that makes it wrong.

Phileo love is a higher type of love. It is the intimate love used in friendships and with companions. It is a love that is very seldom enjoyed by husbands and wives because so few married couples have developed a friendship relationship. Most people (within most marriages) operate from the Eros type of love. The Eros love should be a part of marriage, but the Phileo love should also be a part of marriage. And even beyond the Phileo love, there is another love that God is most concerned with--the Agape love.

The Agape love is the God-kind of love. It is fully expressed in John 3:16 "For God so loved the world, that he gave his only begotten Son, that whosoever believeth in him should not perish, but have everlasting life." Agape is the type of love that moves in your direction when you don't do anything to deserve it. That's the love which God portrayed when He laid down His life for us: "But God commendeth his love toward us, in that, while we were yet sinners, Christ died for us" (Romans 5:8).

Love is...

> *Love is patient, love is kind. It does not envy, it does not boast, it is not proud. It is not rude, it is not self-seeking, it is not easily angered, it keeps no record of wrongs. Love does not delight in evil but rejoices with the truth. It always protects, always trusts, always hopes, always perseveres. Love never fails....*

1 Corinthians 13:4-8 (NIV)

Many men have problems knowing what love really is. To understand what love is, it helps to understand what it is not.

Love is not preferring yourself above your wife. When you come home after a hard day at work and don't lift a finger to assist your wife with the remainder of the household duties, that is not love. When you send your body through the door but your mind is elsewhere, that is not love. When you ask, "What's for dinner," then put your feet up, watch TV and wait until it's ready, that's not love. A man moving in love will understand that his wife has been busy all day, too. While he worked outside the home, she worked within it--cooking, cleaning, washing, drying, and caring for the children. And because what she did was as important as what he did (and even more so!), he will show his regard for her by helping her. If you fail to do this, you will repel your wife. When you walk in the bedroom later and say, "Hey, baby," she'll scream at you to get away.

Men need to learn the law of reciprocity. It says that for every action there is an equal reaction. In other words, what you sow is what you reap. If you want a certain reaction from your wife, you have to perform a certain action toward her. A woman is made to be responsive to a man's actions. Instead of coming home and retreating into your own world, a man should say something like, "Well, darling, did you have a good day?" But many men haven't learned this yet. No man sat down and taught them that women are emotional creatures. Some men found it out after marriage, but many still haven't learned this lesson. Because your wife is an emotional creature, some days she has highs, and some days she has lows. She has children that will cause her moods to fluctuate, and a physical system that cycles once a month. Men must understand this and move in an awareness of it.

As opposed to women, men are physical beings. Men relate to the physical; that is why they like the outdoors so much. Most women have less of an interest in camping, hunting, fishing, and sports than men do. Men respond to these things because of the physical side of their nature. If you plan to get married, you need to understand this difference between men and women, because your spouse is not going to change. Men have not been taught how to make love to a woman. They often look at the Rambo-type of characters on TV and establish their view of love making from this macho point of view (again, we're talking about the physical side of man). If you look at all these tough guys and see the rough things they do and think this is the way to treat women, you're going to have a problem. The displayed sexuality and exploitation of women that is shown on TV has given men the wrong concept of women. And men are walking around in the church with this same nonsense in their minds.

Do you know what you have to do with a woman? You must love her. You can show a woman you love her by buying her candy or flowers. You can also say "I love you" by making a phone call or sending a telegram. A woman would value an "I love you" coming from your heart more than flowers or candy; those things alone won't move her. It's okay to do those things--women do like them. But in addition to that, she'd rather have your arms around her; she'd rather you sit down intimately and make love to her mind.

I've bought candy, jewelry, and clothes and my wife did not respond to any of it. I remember telling her one day, "I'm out working in the church all day and night, trying to provide a better life for you." She responded, "You're working for yourself. We can go back to a small house; I'll take you with a small house." She was revealing something to me about women--women don't value material things as much as they value knowing that they are truly loved and appreciated. Since this takes us back to the role of a sacrificial lover, let's look at this role again.

Sacrificial love is the type of love that Christ exhibits to His church. It is not a responsive love to the actions of the church; it is a love we receive in spite of our actions. Have you always done what Jesus desired you to do? Since we would all have to answer "No," we are acknowledging that we've been in rebellion (which is sin) at some time or another. Yet our actions have not stopped Jesus from loving us. Our actions have not stopped Him from healing us, delivering us, or moving in our direction. This is sacrificial love. It flows in spite of the actions of others. Even when we are cold and indifferent, or rebellious against the revealed will of God, Jesus still does not deny us Himself; He continues to demonstrate His love towards us. It is this type of love, sacrificial love, that the husband should demonstrate towards his wife. Just as Jesus does not expect perfection from the church, the husband cannot expect perfection from his wife. In the Scripture, the wife is likened unto the church. So even when she falls short of the mark, the Lord still expects us to love our wives.

Accountability

God holds the husband responsible for the marriage. God expects a husband to be a man and the leader of his house. God holds the man responsible for changes in the household. If the marriage fails, God holds him accountable.

If there's one thing I don't like, it's henpecked men. And I'm not alone--God doesn't like them either! You see, God can't use henpecked men the way He would like to, because they can't move in the role He has created for them; they won't accept their accountability. Here's a cute, little story that illustrates that point: After the rapture of the church, Gabriel, the archangel, makes this statement in the presence of the saints: "All of the men that were henpecked stand over here." All of the men went to the henpecked side, except for one. One little, short man stood by himself. Gabriel walked over to him and said, ''Do you mean to tell me that out of all the men in the earth, you were the only man who wasn't henpecked? How in the world could you be the head of your family, when all the other men failed?'' The man responded, ''I don't know. My wife just told me to stand over here.'' Now that's a humorous story, but it's making a very serious point. There is no place in the kingdom of God for henpecked men. It is not possible for such men to function in their headship position, to move in the authority that God has given them; men cannot accept their accountability when they are henpecked.

One of the problems with America today is that we have so many weak men. Too many men think that putting on a pair of pants is what makes them men. But there are too many guys putting on pants and acting like girls. These are not necessarily homosexuals, they're just weak men. They won't stand up for anything, and they don't stand for anything. The Bible teaches men to be strong. I don't like weak men; there will be no weak men in authority in my church. And I have found that I can tell the strength of a man by looking at his wife. I look at her and I listen to what she says. I know that if a man can't handle his wife, he can't handle the things of God. Joshua said, ''...but as for me and my house, we will serve the Lord'' (Joshua 24:15). This should be the principle that godly men operate by.

Jesus is the head of the church. He delegates authority to men to function as the heads in their homes. This results in their accountability. The man's job is to call his family together for prayer and to seek the face of the Lord. Then he is to function in that home as a sacrificial lover.

The problem with most men is they have too much ''loving'' on their minds. Physical love will never solve your problems; that's not where sacrificial love begins. Now while it's true that the marriage bed is undefiled (and that's if you're married. If you're unmarried, you shouldn't be involved in a sexual relationship. It's a sin and God will judge it.), that which is beautiful, holy, and righteous in the bed is a product of that which has already been birthed outside the bed. How can you be intimate if the two of you can't even talk to one another?

It reminds me of a theology dean at the Bible college I attended some years back. He said he was a great speaker who preached some great sermons. He would run a revival and then come home and say to his wife, "Honey, so many people got saved; so many people got delivered!" And his wife would say, "Well, how much money do you have? The rent has to be paid and your son needs shoes." (We have to learn not to overspiritualize things.) Then he'd ask his wife, "What have you been doing all day, honey? What's all this dirt on the floor? And the dishes are dirty, too." "Praying down heaven," she'd reply. Neither one of these people were balanced. He should have been a good provider as well as a preacher. She should have been a good homemaker as well as a prayer warrior.

We are accountable for the roles which God has assigned us to. And as it pertains to the man especially, the Bible declares in 1 Timothy 3:5, "For if a man know not how to rule his own house, how shall he take care of the church of God?" You've got no business running around preaching or attempting to minister in the things of God while neglecting your family.

Spiritual Agreement

Can two walk together, except they be agreed?

Amos 3:3

The principle of agreement touches every area of our lives. It becomes especially important when we are dealing with spiritual matters. Your progress in God will be greatly impeded if you allow yourself to be joined to someone who does not have the same spiritual revelation that you do. God will not join you to such a person. It's important that we understand how necessary it is to operate in spiritual agreement. We should be teaching it to our children before they begin to date, so that they will know what choices to make.

By the time my daughter, Rachelle, was thirteen, I had already observed the young teenage boys in our church ministry. I recognized those who were full of the Holy Ghost, and I began to pray that one of those young men, who was on fire for God, would be the mate for my daughter. I knew that if her mate came from our ministry I would have a chance to watch him, and I would know if he was in spiritual agreement with her; I would know if he knew right from wrong. And this is what fathers should be doing as they watch over all the affairs of their household. Yet there are many men who don't understand this, because they've never been taught this principle.

There used to be a time when a boy who wanted to date a girl had to go through the father; there was no such thing as taking out a girl if you hadn't met her father. This was a dating ritual that all young men expected. It was taken for granted that if you wanted to get to the girl, you had to go through her father. This gave him a chance to see if the guy was someone he would approve of for his daughter. Christian parents today must be aware of who their children are keeping company with, and if you detect spiritual incompatibility, it is your duty to break it up before it goes any further. Don't sit by idly and let your children do whatever they want. God will not only hold you responsible, but you will inevitably pay a price for your neglect. Many times when children make the wrong choices the burden falls upon the parents. You do not want to be found in that type of situation.

Godly Men

> *The wicked flee when no man pursueth: but the righteous are bold as a lion.*
>
> Proverbs 28:1

> *...let the weak say, I am strong.*
>
> Joel 3:10

> *...when I am weak, then am I strong.*
>
> 2 Corinthians 12:10

Godly men are strong men. They are fearless, because they know who their God is. They have an intimate, personal relationship with God which makes them bold. Everything reproduces after its own kind. As you love God, He loves you back. And He begins to express Himself to you through His Spirit. This is a life-changing experience. As God opens up your knowledge and understanding, He will give you instructions on how to run your home. This type of husband is the desire of every godly woman. Women are looking for sacrificial lovers, but they also need their husbands to be secure and confident in who they are in God. Just because a person speaks in tongues, it does not mean he is the image of Christ. If he's insecure and has no confidence he is not sent by God. If he can't love himself, he won't be able to love a wife. And because the husband is to love the wife as his own body (Ephesians 5:26), a woman should not accept this type of a man.

Godly Love

> *That he might present it to himself a glorious church, not having spot, or wrinkle, or any such thing; but that it should be holy and without blemish.*

> *So ought men to love their wives as their own bodies. He that loveth his wife loveth himself.*

> *For no man ever yet hated his own flesh; but nourisheth and cherisheth it, even as the Lord the church.*

> Ephesians 5:27-29

Husbands, in order for you to love your wife with the God-kind of love, the Agape love, your relationship with God must be right. You must have an intimate, personal relationship with God so that He will be allowed to flow through you (Agape) to your wife. Every woman on the face of the earth is uniquely different. God will show you how to love your wife. Don't make the mistake of comparing your wife with another woman. It doesn't matter if it's your mother, sister, or friend--women are too unique to be compared with one another. Just let God show you how to love your wife. Loving your wife has to be a quality decision on your part. Husbands must recognize (as must wives) that their first ministry is to their mate, and their household. Your home should reflect the life of Christ, the love that He demonstrated.

Agape love is a demonstrated love. God expressed this love through the act of giving Himself on behalf of His church. He did not base His love on the church's response. When God demonstrated His love toward us through Christ's death, there was nothing we did to merit it. Now God is saying that the husband is to love his wife with the same kind of love.

If you love your wife with Agape love, and work at your marriage, your wife will be pure and holy. She will respond to you in the pattern that the church is supposed to respond to the Lord. As you and your wife become one, you ought to love, cherish, and nourish her as your own body.

The Glory of the Man

...the woman is the glory of the man.

1 Corinthians 11:7

Because she is his glory, a husband should take care of his wife in the same way that he takes care of himself. A husband must nourish and cherish his wife, meeting all her needs.

The husband should make sure his wife looks good, because she is his glory. Make sure you take care of her on the same level as you do yourself. Make her feel like she is the only woman in this earth. Say those three famous words, "I love you," in as many ways as you can. By doing these things for your wife, you will build her up and strengthen her; you will cause her to release herself to you and be a better wife.

Women, on the other hand, have only their hair as their glory. So since you know that, you should see to it that she goes to the beauty shop. You should give her money and tell her, "Honey, you can get anything you want done at the hair salon." Since she's your glory, wouldn't you want her to glorify you? This is part of the mystery of the church. Jesus is the head and we are His body. The only way He can be glorified in the earth is through His body. Likewise, the only way the husband can be glorified is through his wife. The more you express yourself to your wife, the more her beauty will be released; this will be to your glory. Give your wife the time and attention she needs, and she will become all you need her to be.

<u>Are you willing to die?</u>

> *And Jesus answered them, saying, "The hour is come, that the Son of man should be glorified.*
>
> *Verily , verily, I say unto you, Except a corn of wheat fall into the ground and die, it abideth alone: but if it die, it bringeth forth much fruit."*

John 12:23-24

Are you willing to die? If you are ever going to become the person God desires you to be, the answer must be "Yes!" When we offer ourselves to Christ as a living sacrifice, we must make the quality decision to die. This is a dying to self. If too much of ourself remains alive, we will not be able to move in the will of God. If you want God to move in your marriage (or in your single life), you have to die. If you want God to move on your behalf in any way, you must die. Dead people don't do anything--they can't! That's how we must be. Just like when Adam was made completely helpless by God when He put him to sleep and formed Eve, we must become helpless so that God can move on our behalf. Stop trying to make things happen--let God do whatever needs to be done.

The Bible says in Galatians 4:4, ''But when the fulness of the time was come, God sent forth his Son, made of a woman....'' In the fulness of time (when it's time!) your mate is coming. For those of you with unsaved husbands, quit staying up late and pacing the floor, worrying about what that man is doing; forget about it, turn over, and go to sleep. What good is it going to do for you to stay awake worrying and biting your fingernails? You'll be a nervous wreck. Put that man in God's hands--say your prayers then go to sleep. Have a sweet sleep. Then when he awakens the next morning, tell him you love him so much, and prepare his breakfast. You are opening a door for God and closing the door on Satan when you minister to your husband in this way. It is really a dying to self, and an allowing of the love of God to flow through you to your husband. God can work powerfully in such situations. The study of Smith Wigglesworth's salvation is an example of what God can do through a submitted (a dead to self) wife.

Smith Wigglesworth said that before he was saved he drank and did a whole lot of ungodly things. He and his wife had an argument and he told her, ''Don't you go to church. If you go to church, you are not going to get back in here tonight. If you go down to that church again (it was a full gospel church), you are not going to get back in here.'' Mrs. Wigglesworth went anyway. When she returned, she found the door locked. When you begin to believe God, look for the devil. Satan won't make it easy, but keep believing--it will happen! Mrs. Wigglesworth knocked on the door because her key would not fit, but Smith would not answer. So she stood out there all night, speaking in tongues, thanking the Lord Jesus, and praising God. When Smith finally opened the door in the morning, his wife said, ''Good morning, Smith,'' and walked into the house and prepared his breakfast. One month later, Smith Wigglesworth was speaking in tongues. What a testimony to the power of God working through a woman who was dead to self!

Everyone has to die--husbands, wives, and single people. This is the only way God can work. We have to die and allow ourselves to be put into God's hands. Anything we do by voluntary movement is of the flesh, and the flesh only produces flesh. But if we let God do it, the Spirit will make it right. We can't change people; only God can change those who want to be changed. And He does it through those of us who are submitted to Him and dead to self. God can give you a peace; He can fortify you. God's on your side--the side of the righteous. You and God can conquer anybody! No matter who thinks they can beat you, they can't beat God. When you make a decision to put your husband or your wife into the hands of God, He will take care of the situation. We must rememeber that God never brought two people together in marriage for them to separate. If you put your situation in His hands, He will make the difference.

The Waiting Period

While you are waiting for God to work things out on your behalf, He is also doing a work in you. Through the Holy Spirit, He is perfecting the character of Christ in you. God will use the waiting period to get you ready for where He's taking you.

So many women are ''waiting'' for a husband, yet they don't know the first thing about cooking or taking care of a home. And there are brothers who are ''waiting'' for a wife, but they don't even have a job. Brothers, if you don't have a job, you don't need a wife. But this is where the waiting period comes in. God will use the time you call "waiting" to show you some things about yourself. He will help you make the necessary corrections in your life so that when she does come along, you'll be ready. When a man gets married, he is to meet all his wife's needs. When you meet your wife's needs, you will find that she will willingly submit to you in everything.

So the waiting process can actually be a time that God uses to transform you and prepare you for the future He has planned for you. That's exciting!

The Good Shepherd

> *I am the good shepherd: the good shepherd giveth his life for the sheep.*
>
> John 10:11

God commended Agape love towards us, manifested in the form of a human body in the name of Jesus. It was Jesus, the good Shepherd, who laid down His life so that you and I could have a right to the tree of life. Even Jesus had to die in order to bring forth life. Jesus, the good Shepherd, became the sacrificial Lamb and the sacrificial lover. He didn't love us because we were lovable; He took us off the garbage dump of life.

In the same manner that Jesus covers and watches over His church, He is saying to the husband, "Agape your wife." Yet you will never agape your wife without ministering to God. You will never be able to meet the needs of your wife as her sacrificial lover until you come to the place where you die at the altar and God resurrects you. You are never going to receive from God that which He has for you until you first die. In fact, until you die, you're not even going to desire to meet her needs. As long as self is alive, you are going to meet its needs first; that's why it must die.

As the good Shepherd, Jesus gives His all for the church. In the same way, the husband must learn to do this for his wife. Because the wife is a part of him, he must learn to meet all her needs. To neglect her would be to neglect himself (and no man in his right mind would neglect himself).

It's important for men to understand that when they do something nice for themselves, they ought to do something nice for their wife. Whatever you do for yourself should make you think of the needs of your wife, and your family. This is the role of a shepherd--one who watches over and takes care of.

Now lets go back briefly to the roles of the husband and wife. She submits as he moves in the role of a sacrificial lover. A woman will only submit to a man because she loves him. If you operate in these other forms of headship that we talked about, if you're forcing your wife to submit, you're not really a sacrificial lover. And you have no idea what you're missing. It's so wonderful when your wife willingly submits.

Everyone who desires a better marriage should be prepared for death. While God is working on your spouse, do not be moved by what you see; the circumstances are only temporary. Remember that a strong foundation is being built as your spouse takes the word of God and applies it.

Now I'm speaking to the men: Die to self. That's what a sacrificial lover does. He is not a selfish person. There's no way that you are going to meet your wife's needs and yours at the same time. Abandon self. Throw yourself at her feet and say, "Walk on me, baby. I'm determined to meet your needs." That is what Jesus, the good Shepherd, the sacrificial Lamb, did. Jesus said of His life, "No man taketh if from me, but I lay it down of myself" (John 10:18). Brothers, too many of us are still alive. Die and be that rug, if necessary, because through the word, God is building your marriage relationship.

Chapter Ten

The Husband as Provider

But if any provide not for his own, and specially for those of his own house, he hath denied the faith, and is worse than an infidel [an unbeliever or heathen].

1 Timothy 5:8

In writing to Timothy, a bishop over the church in Ephesus, the Apostle Paul makes it very clear that any man who is a believer, and yet fails to take care of his family, is worse than an unbeliever--he has denied the faith.

The word worse means "bad, evil, harmful, unpleasant, and inferior." A husband who does not provide for his own house is harmful and unpleasant to them; he brings evil upon his house; he causes his house to be inferior. When Paul said that such a man "hath denied the faith," he is saying that by his own actions, this man is stating that he's never received the grace of the Gospel; in other words, he is a sinner. No man can sit in the church, claim to be saved, say that he is a worshipper of God, and yet refuse to take care of his own household. Brother, if this description fits you, you are lost. If you're a man who doesn't take care of your own children, you are lost. But God has made a way for you to recover yourself from the snare of the enemy--just line up with His word!

The Lord spoke to me and told me to declare this truth. He said, "Son, you declare this truth. There are men in every church who had children or seed in the earth before they were born-again. Even though they have received salvation and the baptism of the Holy Spirit they are living a lie, because they have children in this earth that they have denied." God is saying that until you go back and get that little boy or girl that you've fathered, your seed in the earth, and take care of your responsibility to them, He will not honor you as a son.

Many men are living a deceived life. You have children in this earth, have remarried, and you've never told your wife that you have other children. Several years back, a young man joined our church. He could speak very eloquently and I was really pleased and enthused about him. Then one day I was told that he had been arrested on his job for not paying child support. His new wife knew nothing of his child until that moment. You can imagine what happened in that relationship. But that wasn't all. Soon a second child, and then a third were attributed to this man. And in the eyes of God, he was accountable for all of them. Men, when we were sinners, we did a lot of things in the earth that we shouldn't have. And it's true that when we are saved, God forgives us for all our sins. But if you've fathered any children in the earth, God does not release you from your responsibility of providing for them.

The Bible says that Sarah called Abraham "lord," which means provider or protector (Genesis 18:12). Men, you have a moral obligation to take care of your seed. Not only are you to put food on the table, you are also to protect and spiritually lead your family. This might be troubling to some women who have married men that are in these types of situations. But, wives, through the grace of God, if you do what is right, God will honor you; He will work things out for you.

Men are responsible for meeting the needs of their wives. Emotionally, intellectually, physically, and financially, women have needs that must be met. One way in which a man meets his wife's needs is through working. Men are supposed to work. When God put Adam in the garden, He gave him work to do. Work honors God. The Apostle Paul says in 2 Thessalonians 3:10, "...if any would not work, neither should he eat." God is saying that work is good. Work gives the husband a way to provide for his own house. It is not the church's job to provide for his house. It is not even his in-law's or relative's job to provide for his house. The Bible explains that the husband is to provide for his own house. And since the husband is to be the provider, a man has no business getting married if he does not have a job and a means of caring for his wife. Until you can support her, you should not even consider taking a wife.

If you're going to be the provider for your family, you need to understand the word of God. because God's word will show you how to be a provider. The word of God teaches you to pay tithes. It teaches you to give. It tells you how to walk in the counsel of the godly. Through the word of God, you will discover all you need to know to be the provider for your family.

America has promoted the wife leaving the home to work. However, in Scripture God put the man, Adam, in the garden to dress and keep it. The principle of work was established before the fall. Adam would work in the day, and afterwards, in the cool of the evening, God would come down and converse with him. After the fall, God said to Adam, ''In the sweat of thy face shalt thou eat bread...'' (Genesis 3:19). I interpret that to mean that the woman should be in the home and the man should be out working. I know that because of lifestyles and sin, families have been destroyed. Women have had to go into the workplace and provide for their families; and they've done a marvelous job. So many homes today are single-parent homes headed by women. If it wasn't for the grace of God moving in the lives of these women, the children of these families would be worse off than they are. We take our hats off to these mothers, but that does not negate the outline or pattern that God has established. There is something different about a home when the children know that their mother is there, within the house, while the father is working.

God said that the man is to provide. A lot of women that are working outside of the home are not doing so because they have to, but because they want to. We need to examine this, to examine our motives and the price we are paying for living contrary to God's word. Many women work because of their desire to own things. The problem with that is that they are working with the wrong motive. Home and family should take precedence over material things.

Husbands, if your wife works outside the home, don't take her check and pay the mortage. Don't take her check and pay the utility bills. If your wife works outside the home, let it be for something special. Let her save her money and use it to go on a second honeymoon or a vacation, or to buy a piece of furniture or something else she wants. When it comes to paying the mortage, the utilities, and even buying the food, that is the job of the provider, the husband.

When we were first married, my wife was working. She has a Master's Degree in Education and was employed by the Detroit Board of Education. She earned more than $30,000 a year, but after the birth of our son, Jonathan, she came home and never returned. The year she came home, my salary for the whole year was $13,000. But we lived better on that $13,000 than we had ever lived in our marriage.

Money does not mean you are going to have a good marriage. When we first got married, we used to eat fried potatoes and chicken. I drank Vernors and ate fried chicken wings, potatoes, and toast. And I was happy. It would be better for some families to eat peanut butter and jelly than for the women to go out into the workplace.

If a man is willing, there is no reason why he cannot support his wife and family. All he has to do is take the word of God and stand in faith. God will show you how to build for your family. It is your responsibility, men; God is expecting you to learn how to do it.

Subdue and Safeguard

> *And God blessed them, and God said unto them,*
> *Be fruitful, and multiply, and replenish the earth,*
> *and subdue it: and have dominion over the fish of*
> *the sea, and over the fowl of the air, and over every*
> *living thing that moveth upon the earth.*

Genesis 1:28

The word subdue means to bring under subjection. God has given man dominion, but He's telling man that there is something that he has to do in order to bring the earth under subjection. Life comes with a struggle. It's not easy.

> *And the Lord God took the man, and put him into*
> *the garden of Eden to dress it and to keep it.*

Genesis 2:15

The word keep means to guard. Adam was told not only to work and dress the garden, but to guard it as well. He was given dominion, rulership, over everything that moved upon the face of the earth. He was to keep or preserve the garden. Adam had been given divine responsibility; God commissioned him to keep the garden. As a husband and father, there is a wife and children that God has put into your hands. He is charging you to keep them. He has commissioned you because you are going to give an account to God on how you have kept your family.

> *This is a true saying, If a man desire the office of a bishop, he desireth a good work.*
>
> *A bishop then must be blameless, the husband of one wife, vigilant, sober, of good behaviour, given to hospitality, apt to teach;*
>
> *Not given to wine, no striker, not greedy of filthy lucre; but patient, not a brawler, not covetous;*
>
> *One that ruleth well his own house, having his children in subjection with all gravity;*
>
> *(For if a man know not how to rule his own house, how shall he take care of the church of God?)*
>
> 1 Timothy 3:1-5

A bishop is not to follow, but to lead--he rules his own house. This Scripture is not referring to the bishop teaching his own house (and that he should do, as well), but to the fact that he must rule. The man has a divine mandate to oversee the affairs of his house. He must watch over the conduct of his house to make sure that it is correct; God will hold him accountable.

Brothers, God is saying that you should not even think about doing something for Him if you can't run your own house. I've seen numerous ministries destroyed simply because a man couldn't rule his own house.

In this day and time, families are falling apart. And the husbands and wives who are supposed to be spiritual, are blaming each other. There is only one culprit. It's not your wife and it's not your husband. The Bible says, "For we wrestle not against flesh and blood, but against principalities, against powers, against the rulers of the darkness of this world, against spiritual wickedness in high places." (Ephesians 5:12). Your enemy, and my enemy, and the only enemy of every husband and wife, is Satan. He's the only one we should be fighting against!

> *Likewise must the deacons be grave, not doubletongued, not given to much wine, not greedy of filthy lucre;*
>
> *Holding the mystery of the faith in a pure conscience.*
>
> *And let these also first be proved; then let them use the office of a deacon, being found blameless.*
>
> *Even so must their wives be grave, not slanderers, sober, faithful in all things.*
>
> *Let the deacons be the husbands of one wife, ruling their children and their own houses well.*

1 Timothy 3:8-12

The Bible says we are "to know them which labour among you" (1 Thessalonians 5:12). We are to know the qualifications of the men that serve in the church. A man's qualifications are determined by how well he governs his house. If a man can't take care of his house, he can't take care of the house of God. If a man can't restore order in his home, he will never be able to keep order in the house of God. The wife of a man who is in a position of leadership in the church must be in subjection to him. If she is not submitted to him, he cannot expect the people of God to be submitted to him.

<u>Family Relationships</u>

> *And he said, A certain man had two sons:*
>
> *And the younger of them said to his father, Father, give me the portion of goods that falleth to me. And he divided unto them his living.*
>
> *And not many days after the younger son gathered all together, and took his journey into a far country, and there wasted his substance with riotous living.*
>
> *And when he had spent all, there arose a mighty famine in that land; and he began to be in want.*
>
> *And he went and joined himself to a citizen of that country; and he sent him into his fields to feed swine.*
>
> *And he would fain have filled his belly with the husks that the swine did eat: and no man gave unto him.*

And when he came to himself, he said, How many hired servants of my father's have bread enough and to spare, and I perish with hunger!

I will arise and go to my father, and will say unto him, Father, I have sinned against heaven, and before thee,

And am no more worthy to be called thy son: make me as one of thy hired servants.

And he arose, and came to his father. But when he was yet a great way off, his father saw him, and had compassion, and ran, and fell on his neck, and kissed him.

And the son said unto him, Father, I have sinned against heaven, and in thy sight, and am no more worthy to be called thy son.

But the father said to his servants, Bring forth the best robe, and put it on him; and put a ring on his hand, and shoes on his feet:

And bring hither the fatted calf, and kill it; and let us eat, and be merry:

For this my son was dead, and is alive again; he was lost, and is found. And they began to be merry.

Luke 15:11-24

The theme of this parable is family relationships. Jesus often taught through parables, and even though this particular one was directed to the house of Israel, it is applicable to our lives today.

The parable paints a picture of a son and his inheritance. There are biblical principles involved here, so let's look at them.

First of all, the Bible teaches in Proverbs 13:22 that it is the father's responsibility to lay up an inheritance for his children: "A good man leaveth an inheritance to his children's children ...." Every parent should be saving something for their children. (The world has perverted this principle into just the opposite. They teach that the children should provide for their parents. And while it is true that situations may occur where a parent will need a son's or daughter's assistance, this is not a principle that should guide our lives.) God expects you to provide an inheritance for your children.

The second issue here is the time at which the inheritance was usually divided. This did not usually occur until after the father's death. So in this parable we have an unusual situation of the son asking for his inheritance while his father was still living. Something was out of order and it was most likely the son's thinking. (I believe he already had the spirit of rebellion). So the father yielded to his request. Not because it was right (and we need to take note of this--just because we want something, and get it, does not mean it is God's will for us; the consequences may prove that just the opposite was true), but because he no doubt understood the spirit of his son and decided to let him have his way. And this is the way that God deals with us. Sometimes He lets us have our way even when He knows better, because we have positioned ourselves in such a way that this is the only option we allow.

There is another principle at play here. The son was not the son he should have been because he thought too much of himself and his own desires. Men, you are not going to have a good family relationship until you die to self. A lot of us are compromising when what we really need to do is die. You need to lay everyone on the altar--your children, your wife, and especially yourself. The prodigal son's father had this attitude--he was dead to himself. He knew his son was wrong to ask for his inheritance; it was disrupting to the whole family. But he released it to him, and allowed him to go, because he so adamantly desired it. This young man had so positioned himself that there was no other way for him to learn the lesson that laid ahead.

So the prodigal son went out into the world and lived riotously with women, wine, and dancing (just like some of our children do today). And being very unwise, it was not long before he had spent all and had nothing left. When a person is accustomed to reigning in life, when they have no responsibilities, they really don't know how to work and take care of things, even money. So this young man was obviously used to ruling and not working, and he soon found himself in a very bad situation. Eventually he found himself working with the swine in a land where a famine was taking place. This type of work was an abomination to the Jews. Yet this was the place he had come to, because this is the place rebellion will bring you to: you will always wind up on the bottom when you operate in rebellion. But with God there is always hope. This young man went down so that he could come up. Luke 15:17 says, "And when he came to himself...."

God is waiting on all of us to come to the end of ourselves so that He can have His way with us. When we get to that place, we can then arise and go back to the Father. One writer said that when the prodigal son approached the house, the father was looking for him. And that's what God is doing with us--while we're out in our sin, wallowing around in the filth, He's waiting for us, He's looking for us. Even though this son had interrupted the family's inheritance, the father lived in expectation that his son would learn a lesson. Have you ever wondered what possessed the father to believe that the son would even learn a lesson from his experiences? I believe the reason for this father's hope was that he made a spiritual deposit in his son. He had taught him the principles pertaining to the kingdom of God. The Bible says, ''Train up a child in the way he should go: and when he is old, he will not depart from it'' (Proverbs 22:6). Sometimes, when you are young and immature, you will depart. But the key is, you will not depart forever. Proverbs 11:21 says, ''the seed of the righteous shall be delivered.''

If your children are young and wandering, just stand your ground in God. You know what principles you've instilled in them. Stand in God's word and know that they're going to come back! This father was looking for his son to return. But some of us are guilty of not even looking for our children to return. Some of you have daughters who've had children out of wedlock, but you're so self-righteous that instead of looking for them to return, you condemn them. Now, I'm not suggesting that you condone or compromise with sin, but the Bible emphatically teaches that ''charity [love] shall cover the multitude of sins'' (1 Peter 4:8). You're not to deny their sins (or yours either, for that matter); you're to love them.

Some men are so macho and so strong that we don't even know how to love our sons; we don't know what it means to put our arms around them and tell them we love them. Some of our sons are into homosexuality and it's so repulsive to us that we turn from them. Yet, beyond a shadow of a doubt, just as Jesus died for you, He died for your children. I'm by no means telling you to condone homosexuality--it's wrong! But God expects you to be looking for your sons (and daughters) when they turn around. You should be on your face night and day praying to God to turn your children around.

There are also women (and men) who are pro-abortionists. But the Bible teaches that the life of all flesh is in the blood, so this makes abortion wrong. Period. Yet, even though the Bible is very clear on this, some saved fathers have influenced their daughters to have abortions. This is in direct opposition to the Scripture found in 1 Timothy 5:22: "...neither be partaker of other men's sins...." Two wrongs don't make a right. We all grew up with this statement, but do we really believe it?

The prodigal son's father was looking for his son. When the son came to himself and returned home, the father was waiting. He saw him from a far and cried, "That's my son!" He hastened to greet him, calling his servants to minister to him. He told them to put the best clothing on him, and adorn his finger with a ring. He had a party to celebrate --the son who was lost had been found. He who was blind, could now see.

Church, we have something to shout about. We have the truth! There is a purging going on in the body of Christ, and God is doing the purging. He is washing us by the water of His word. Fathers and husbands, we are responsible for teaching this word to our children. We will stand before God in accountability for our family relationships. We must remember that our first ministry is to our families.

Household Authority

Abraham was the father of faith. Let's look at his story and see how God moved in his life, equipping him to command his house with authority.

Now the LORD had said unto Abram, Get thee out of thy country, and from thy kindred, and from thy father's house, unto a land that I will show thee:

And I will make of thee a great nation, and I will bless thee, and make thy name great; and thou shalt be a blessing:

And I will bless them that bless thee, and curse him that curseth thee: and in thee shall all families of the earth be blessed.

Genesis 12:1-3

Abraham was destined to be the head of a great family. Yet before that could happen, he had to yield to the will of God in his life and allow a divine repositioning to take place. The psalmist declares that the word of God (His truth) is a shield and a buckler to the believer (Psalm 91:4). When God first spoke to Abraham (when he was still known as Abram), he didn't know God, but he took that word God spoke and used it to reorder his life. And the first thing he had to do was to yield control of his family to God. As Abraham found grace to yield to the will of God, his relationship with God deepened.

And the Lord said, Shall I hide from Abraham that thing which I do;

Seeing that Abraham shall surely become a great and mighty nation, and all the nations of the earth shall be blessed in him?

For I know him, that he will command his chil-

dren and his household after him, and they shall
keep the way of the Lord, to do justice and judg-
ment; that the Lord may bring upon Abraham that
which he hath spoken of him.

Genesis 18:17-19

As Abraham continued to walk with the Lord, God
came to know him as a man who commanded his household
well. And this is the legacy for every saved man today. God
is expecting you to use the authority He has given you and
command your households well. And He is making provision
for you to do that. When you walk in agreement with the Lord,
He reveals things to you. Wouldn't you like to be in the
position where God talks to you about things before He does
them (Amos 3:7)? This is His will and purpose for you.

When God testified of Abraham, He said, "I chose
Abraham out of all the men in the earth because I know he's
going to teach his children and his grandchildren." Did you
catch that? Children and grandchildren. God is not only
concerned with how you raise your children; your job doesn't
stop there. He also expects your parenting ministry to extend
to your grandchildren. It's your job to assist in teaching them
the things of God.

And one last word on household authority: Men, you
are responsible for everyone in your house and everything that
goes on in your household. That includes whoever is living
with you, whether it is your in-laws, other relatives, or anyone
else. Whoever comes under your roof must come under your
rule. So this lets you know that when you have guests staying
in your home, and their stay occurs over the nights when you
have church, you must set the tone. You should not only
continue to go to church with the rest of your household, you

should insist that your guests come, too. Serving God is part of your life and all who come to stay in your home must understand and honor that. There is no other way for a godly man moving in the authority of God to operate.

Precept and Example

If you are going to teach (or train) a child, there are two primary principles that you should keep in mind: you must teach by precept and example. The problem with the church and with religious people is that we talk a good game but do nothing. You cannot tell your child, ''Do what I say,'' and then practice the opposite. Children will perceive this and you will wind up with a big problem. It's the same way with preachers who say, ''Don't do what I do; just do what I tell you to do.'' What nonsense! Jesus said, ''And what I say unto you I say unto all'' (Mark 13:37). Jesus made no special rules, no exclusionary clauses, for adults and preachers. Every person in the church, every member of the body of Christ, is expected to uphold the same standard. That standard is the life of Christ. Everything Jesus taught, He lived. Without exception. We must do the same.

If you're going to teach your children to walk in love, you must walk in love yourself. If you're going to tell your child to pray for a certain amount of time each day, then you should spend at least that much time in prayer. If you're going to tell your child that you believe God for your healing, then you ought to stand on that. Don't forget it at the first sign of symptoms. Teach your children by standing for your healing. Live this thing before them. It will make all the difference. You should be an example of what you teach, because what you live is what's going to be reproduced in your children.

And while you're training your children, teach them to

respect the house of God. (I also have children, so I'm not excluding myself from this admonition.) So many of our children are undisciplined in the house of God. They come to church and act like they have had no upbringing. This is a shame to families and to the church. Ask God to lead you into a better way.

The Promise

> *And there was a famine in the land, beside the first famine that was in the days of Abraham. And Isaac went unto Abimelech king of the Philistines unto Gerar.*
>
> Genesis 26:1

Men need to know that it is not God's will for His people, the church to go to the world for help. As the authority figure in your home, the first thing you must do when your family has a need is to '' let your request be made known unto God'' (Philippians 4:6). Before you go to your pastor or any other church member, go to God.

> *And the Lord appeared unto him, and said, Go not down into Egypt; dwell in the land which I shall tell thee of: sojourn in this land, and I will be with thee, and will bless thee; for unto thee, and unto thy seed, I will give all these countries, and I will perform the oath which I sware unto Abraham thy father.*
>
> Genesis 26:2-3

Isaac was activating the promise that God had given to

his father, Abraham. God spoke to Abraham and Abraham in turn told Isaac the promise. Then when Isaac began to respond to the circumstances before him, the famine, the word that Abraham had planted in him began to rise up. Are you aware that circumstances are subject to change, that they are temporal? But the word of God never changes; God never changes. There is no shadow of turning in Him. If He spoke it, it will come to pass. So Isaac stood on the word. And he was also standing on the example that Abraham had lived before him. Because of what he saw as Abraham walked with God, he believed God would help him. Remember, it is the word and the example that make the difference.

> *And I will make thy seed to multiply as the stars of heaven, and will give unto thy seed all these countries; and in thy seed shall all the nations of the earth be blessed;*
>
> *Because that Abraham obeyed my voice, and kept my charge, my commandments, my statutes, and my laws.*
>
> *And Isaac dwelt in Gerar...*
>
> *Then Isaac sowed in that land, and received in the same year an hundredfold: and the LORD blessed him.*
>
> *And the man waxed great, and went forward, and grew until he became very great:*
>
> *For he had possession of flocks, and possession of herds, and great store of servants: and the Philistines envied him.*
>
> Genesis 26: 4-6;12-14

Who are the Philistines today? They are the unbelievers, the ungodly. There is the voice or counsel that God tells
us not to walk in, not to listen to. God blessed Abraham
because he obeyed His voice, keeping His statues and judgments. Abraham was a doer of the word and he taught his
children to do likewise. As fathers, we are to be epistles,
written and read by all men (2 Corinthians 3:2). We ought to
be examples of what we teach so that when we teach our
children the way of the Lord, they will believe it.

Abraham must have discussed the promise with Isaac.
He must have prepared Isaac to receive it, telling him that he
was the promised seed, given miraculously by God. The
promises of God are very important. We must do everything
within our power to convey them to our children because the
promises of God are what they will be able to stand on.

Dwelling with Knowledge

*Likewise, ye husbands, dwell with them according
to knowledge, giving honour unto the wife, as
unto the weaker vessel, and as being heirs together of the grace of life; that your prayers be not
hindered.*

1 Peter 3:7

Husbands, you must understand delegated authority in
order to fulfill this scripture. Even though you are responsible
for the marital relationship, your wife is an heir with you of
the grace of life. You are to minister to her from the word of
God to keep her pure. In the physical sense, you are to meet

all of her needs because she is considered to be the weaker vessel (even though society promotes the lie that she's as much of a man as you are).

Husbands, you must dwell with your wives according to knowledge. Your wife has nothing to do with your mother, your aunt, or any other woman so you can't dwell with her through a knowledge of them; you dwell with her according to who she is. You may be used to doing things a certain way for your mother, even buying her certain gifts, but that won't work with your wife; she's a different woman and you have to understand that.

I remember after Vickey and I married, I realized I didn't like the cologne she was wearing. But instead of buying a cologne that I knew another woman liked (like my mother or my aunt), I bought her ten different fragrances and placed them under the Christmas tree. She was then free to choose from among them (it didn't matter to me because I liked them all!), and she wasn't restricted by another woman's choice.

Oftentimes, that is where men make their mistake. They see something on another woman and assume it is the thing to buy for their wife. Watch out, brothers; you're asking for trouble. Women are too different to deal with them like that. Your wife is your wife, and you want to learn about her. Make it your constant goal. It requires some experimentation, but when you finally get it right, it is well worth the effort.

You have to be consistent and constantly go back over the drawing board. God made women with the ability to change often. You need to watch your wife each day to see how she is, what mood she's in, and how you can best minister to her. This is dwelling according to knowledge. Not forcing her to be one way all the time. That's impossible and it is not God's way! You must understand her tendency to change moods, and learn to work with her. You don't want your prayers to be hindered, so you have to learn this principle (1 Peter 3:7). And learning to be your wife's husband can be quite a revelation.

I remember waking up one morning around 2:00 a.m. I went downstairs and began to pray and worship the Lord. Then the Lord began to minister to me, to break me down. I began to cry out to Him, saying "Lord, I'm not the husband-man I want to be. Everything you want me to be, I want to be." You see, when I stand before people to teach them about the things of God, I'm not just teaching something for excitement or to be humorous--I'm dealing with life issues. I want a good marriage and I want everyone in my assembly to have a good marriage. I want to set an example. And so God must deal with me first. I must first understand how to dwell with my wife according to knowledge before I can teach others.

Perfect Love

So I continued to pray, "Lord, you gave me this Scripture about Sarah obeying Abraham (1 Peter 3:6), now give me revelation and understanding concerning it." (I really didn't know what the Lord was going to say.) I waited on Him and He began to minister to me: "Son, do you remember when you read in Genesis that Abraham is a fine example of a believer who was yet not in obedience to the word?" (Abraham was bound by fear when he went into Egypt.) Yet the Bible says, "..perfect love casteth out fear: because fear hath torment" (1 John 4:18).

When you read Abraham's story, it becomes evident that he was not walking in this perfect love; in fact, he was walking in fear. And it is very important for men to realize that when they are not walking in perfect love, when they are instead walking in fear, they will fail their wives and families.

God has great plans for the marital relationship. He has ordained it to be successful in every way. In the same way that He framed the worlds by His word, every marriage, and every home, can be framed in the God-kind of relationship. We only have to take Him at His word.

Chapter Eleven

Divorce and Remarriage

And he answered and said unto them, Have ye not read, that he which made them at the beginning made them male and female,

And said, For this cause shall a man leave father and mother, and shall cleave to his wife: and they twain shall be one flesh?

Wherefore they are no more twain, but one flesh. What therefore God hath joined together, let not man put asunder.

They say unto him, Why did Moses then command to give a writing of divorcement, and to put her away?

He saith unto them, Moses because of the hardness of your hearts suffered you to put away your wives: but from the beginning it was not so.

Matthew 19:4-8

The Pharisees were tempting Jesus. ''Is it lawful for a man to put his wife away for every cause?'', they asked. In His answer, Jesus took them back to the beginning of God's creation. He was not going to deal in theology, doctrines, dogmas, teachings, or commandments of men; Jesus took them back to God's original intention for marriage.

The Pharisees were accustomed to men putting their wives away for any and every cause. And moving within their own rules and laws, the Pharisees sanctioned this. But they were far from God's will on the matter.

Today, we live in the same type of society. Men and women alike disregard marriage, failing to esteem it for the sacred covenant that God designed it to be.

Thus saith the Lord, Stand ye in the ways, and see, and ask for the old paths, where is the good way, and walk therein, and ye shall find rest for your souls. But they said, We will not walk therein.

Jeremiah 6:16

In Christendom, there are many voices, doctrines, organizations, and human personalities that are speaking to the church. It is very rare that you hear a clear, unadulterated word from the Lord. Yet the Bible tells us to ''try the spirits whether they are of God'' (1 John 4:1). Whether you know it or not, out of all the voices in the earth today, God's voice remains the same. He still says what He means and means what He says regarding the marriage covenant.

Remember ye the law of Moses my servant, which I commanded unto him in Horeb for all Israel, with the statutes and judgments.

Malachi 4:4

In speaking to the house of Judah, before heaven was closed up for approximately 400 years, God said, ''Remember ye the laws of Moses my servant.'' These were one of the last words God spoke to them. After that, there was no clear word from the Lord for 400 years. God was telling them that the information they needed to know in order to be successful had already been delivered to His servant Moses; they needed to hear what he had said. And I'm saying today that the reason so many within the body of Christ are not prospering is because they have left the word of God and followed the voice of strangers. What you need to know to be successful in the things of God has already been written. Learn it and follow it!

The church of God must make the quality decision to respond in obedience when we hear the word of God. It amazes me how saints have been misled. In today's times, a pastor can stand and declare the truth and people will say, ''He's stepping on my toes!'' Do you think the pastor should be tickling your toes? And he's not doing it anyway. It is the word that has found you out. It is conviction. That is what makes you feel so unpleasant. The word of God comes to change you. The Bible says it's sharper than a two-edged sword (Hebrews 4:12). Doesn't it make sense that it will hurt you sometimes? The other part of the truth is that the word of God also comes to bless you, to build you up, to enlighten you, and to give you direction by freeing you. The word does not come to put you in bondage.

The Fornication Clause

And I say unto you, Whosoever shall put away his wife, except it be for fornication, and shall marry another, committeth adultery: and whoso marrieth her which is put away doth commit adultery.

Matthew 19:9

Satan has always attempted to pervert the word of God, and this passage of scripture has not escaped his attack. When Jesus arrived on the scene, the controversy surrounding divorce and remarriage had already been raging. In fact, we have record of a debate over the issue since the days of Moses.

Hillel and Shammai, two prominent Jewish Rabbis, held opposing views on the issue of divorce and remarriage. Hillel held that a man could divorce his wife for "any" reason, or "every" cause. Think about it: you name it, and you could become a free man because of it. Let's say, for example, that your wife was not the best housekeeper--her standards didn't measure up to yours. Solution: get rid of her. Never mind about discussing the situation and trying to work things out. This is your opportunity to get rid of her, get a new wife (maybe even a younger, more beautiful one) and start over. Why not? After all, Hillel said you can divorce her for "every" cause. The problem with this way of thinking is that it is not God-centered; this is not what Jesus taught.

Contained within the teachings of Shammai is the doctrine that our Lord Jesus put forth. Shammai's interpretation of the law caused him to teach that a man could only divorce his wife for the sin of fornication. He was correct, and Jesus picked up on this when He came, making it very clear in the book of Matthew: God allows divorce only for the reason of fornication (yet there is one other instance that frees the believer; we'll discuss it later in this chapter). If people divorce for reasons other than this, and remarry, God considers it an act of adultery. Let's define fornication, so we can have a clear understanding of it.

Simply put, fornication means sexual immorality. Fornication covers any sexual sins, including homosexuality and beastiality. God will allow the innocent party to terminate the marriage covenant in the face of these sins. He releases them from all marital obligations and allows them to start a new life, with remarriage if they choose. That's how serious God considers such violations of the marriage covenant. And God has always felt this way about marriage.

Under the Mosaic law, adultery was a crime punishable by death. If a woman was found in an adulterous relationship, she was stoned to death (along with the man; Leviticus 20:10). Divorce wasn't the solution--death was! That's how serious God considers the sin of adultery, and how highly He regards the marriage covenant. He won't let it be dissolved for just any reason. We need to wake up and get with God's program. God wants us to understand that divorce is usually predicated upon one reason--hardness of the heart. He wants us to realize that in most cases, if you get your heart right with God, your marriage can be saved. Notice I said in most cases. There will always be the exception. We must remember that we serve a God of grace.

God is dealing with issues of the heart. Oftentimes, when people get hurt, they do not know how to deal with those hurts. As a result, they suppress them. When people do not deal with them quickly, their hearts become hardened. Once their hearts harden, penetration becomes difficult if not impossible. In other words, they can no longer be reached by His word. So in the case of marital difficulties, these people are ready to put away their marriage partners (both men and women) rather than have their hearts changed by the word of God. But the word of God is teaching something different. And that is what we have to understand. If a person releases their hurts to God, and gets their heart right before God, they will never entertain divorce, or even separation. In Proverbs 4:23, the word of the Lord says, "Keep thy heart with all diligence; for out of it are the issues of life." It's an issue of the heart.

Let's take sin, for example. Sin is a decision of the heart. In other words, the manifestation of sin in a person's life reveals what has already taken place in the heart. So in the case of adultery, Jesus explained that the adulterous act does not begin with what you see in the physical realm--it was first conceived in the heart. Jesus taught that "whosoever looketh on a woman to lust after her hath committed adultery with her already in his heart" (Matthew 5:28). It's the heart. There is a constant battle going on for our heart: Satan is trying to get control of it, and God demands control of it. God looks at the heart (1 Samuel 16:7). If anyone can "see right through you," it is God. For this reason, we must guard our hearts.

The reason so many believers do not enjoy God's utopia or zenith in marriage is simply because they think it is primarily a physical union. This is a false concept of marriage. Certainly there is a physical component, but that part was designed to be an outward manifestation of the inward union. Marriage is a spiritual union. If we ever truly realize this, our marriages will receive new life and take on new meaning. The selfishness that so often dominates marital unions will fall away.

And that's what Jesus was trying to get the people to see as He taught them about divorce. Separation and divorce is essentially an act of selfishness. It is a person saying, "I want my needs met rather than the will of God being done in my life." I know it is hard for us to see sometimes, but God's way is so much better than ours.

> *When a man hath taken a wife, and married her, and it come to pass that she find no favour in his eyes, because he hath found some uncleanness in her: then let him write her a bill of divorcement, an give it in her hand, and send her out of his house.*

And when she is departed out of his house, she may go and be another man's wife.

And if the latter husband hate her, and write her a bill of divorcement, and giveth it in her hand, and sendeth her out of his house; or if the latter husband die, which took her to be his wife;

Her former husband, which sent her away, may not take her again to be his wife, after that she is defiled;for that is an abomination before the Lord: and thou shalt not cause the land to sin, which the Lord thy God giveth thee for an inheritance.

Deuteronomy 24:1-4

I put this passage of Scripture here to drive home the point that divorce was granted because of the hardness of the people's hearts. It came through Moses, and God permitted it, but from the beginning it was not so. Divorce itself is a sin to the guilty party, and it is not the will of God. However, it is not the unpardonable sin.

The Unbeliever's Departure

I mentioned earlier that there is one other instance in which the believer is freed from the covenant of marriage. Let's read about it in 1 Corinthians 7:15:

But if the unbelieving depart, let him depart. A brother or a sister is not under bondage in such cases: but God hath called us to peace.

The first thing we must do as we approach this passage of Scripture, is to interpret it in the time in which it was written; we must keep it in it's context to avoid misunderstanding. At the time Paul wrote this word to the Corinthian church, Corinth was plagued by a high level of idolatry and paganism. In this type of situation, the Apostle Paul felt it was necessary to address the issue of spousal desertion. Many of those who renounced their pagan practices and became Christians, were still married to people steeped in the practice of idolatrous worship. Undoubtedly, many were converted by their Christian spouses, but from the need Paul felt to write this Scripture, we can be sure that many were not. As they continued in their polluted practices, they operated without regard for the beliefs of their Christian spouses. As the husband or wife was washed by the word of God and became unpolluted from the things of the world, many of them were rejected by their unbelieving spouses. These were polluted people, rejecting the living God and those who served Him. In this type of situation, God released the Christian partner from the marriage bonds.

In applying this truth to our lives today, we must be sensitive to the truth of God's word. Most of our spouses are not polluted by idol worship or practicing paganism. In fact, most partners in most marriages will confess that they believe in God, even if one of them is not born-again. So what we have in our society at large today, is much confession of Christianity with oftentimes little practice of it. If you are a believer who has been deserted by your spouse, you must seek the will of God concerning your situation. God's chief interest in marriages is to save them, not dissolve them. But if your unbelieving husband or wife chooses to leave you, and wants nothing more to do with you as a marriage partner because of your Christian beliefs which have produced a Christian lifestyle, according to the truth of God's word you are free.

I would like to leave you with this thought: no matter how good you think your marriage is, every marriage goes through rough spots. Because Satan wants to destroy every marriage, it is at those times that he will attempt to plant thoughts of separation and divorce in your mind. That's when you have to be certain that God never intended for there to be separation or divorce. If you fasten on to the word of God in those difficult times, the most likely thing that will happen is that God will restore your marriage to a better state than it ever was before. But this will require persistence and a made-up mind on your part. If you are willing, God will work wonders in your marriage. It is what He wants to do.

Chapter Twelve

Sowing and Reaping

Be not deceived; God is not mocked [God will not be laughed at or scorned]: for whatsoever a man soweth, that shall he also reap.

For he that soweth to his flesh shall of the flesh reap corruption; but he that soweth to the Spirit shall of the Spirit reap life everlasting.

And let us not be weary in well doing: for in due season we shall reap, if we faint not.

Galatians 6:7-9

The word ''soweth'' in this passage of Scripture means to plant. And the word ''whatsoever'' means just that-- whatever or anything you want. Jesus is teaching that you have the right to plant in the earth whatever you want to. He is saying that as far as the return you want, you will get the desired results based on what you plant. This is a profound spiritual principle that can and should be applied to the marriage relationship. If you want not only a good marriage, but the God-kind of marriage, you have to plant to receive the right type of mate. If you don't plant what you want, you cannot expect to receive what you want.

The word ''reap'' as used here, means to come forth, or to give back. As was typical of His teaching methods, Jesus was using a natural event to explain a spiritual principle. The earth gives back that which has been planted. All truth is parallel. In the natural, if you plant peas, you will reap peas; if you plant corn, you will harvest corn; if it's tomatoes, then you get tomatoes. It is a natural principle that cannot be altered: you will always reap what you sow. But there is another very important point contained within this sowing and reaping principle: you will always reap more than what you plant. And just as it is in the natural, so too in the spiritual realm. God always gives back more than what we plant. This is the principle of multiplication.

Ephesians 3:20 says, ''Now unto him that is able to do exceeding abundantly above all that we ask or think, according to the power that worketh in us....'' God is so far beyond us in His method of operation; we really need to come to the place where we better understand that. The reason most people don't understand God's mode of operation is because they don't read their Bibles, so they don't see the word in operation. These people have never had godly examples while growing up. To comprehend that God's word is energized with His very life and nature is beyond them; they really can't grasp it. Yet the word of God is alive and able to do great things in the life of all His people. It is God's will that we understand this.

If you take that which is life, the word of God, and plant it in good ground, you can determine what and how much you will get back. This is why some people receive a thirtyfold blessing while others received a hundredfold return. It also explains why some women marry ''half-saved,'' lukewarm men--the men are products of what they've planted! They are reaping what they have sown. You cannot expect a man who is a spiritual giant to walk into your life if you have been sowing seeds of disobedience. Nor can you expect a man who is a doer of the word, if you've been a hearer only.

Every marriage needs some type of improvement to reach the zenith or apex of what God has intended for marriage from the beginning. Good marriages just don't happen. They take work, and a lot of it. In fact, the person who tells you that marriage is a 50/50 relationship, is deceived. If you're only giving a fifty percent effort in your marriage, and your spouse is only giving fifty percent too, the marriage is doomed to fail. Marriage takes a 100 percent effort on the part of both people. It's not something you can succeed at by working sparingly; you must work continuously in order to be successful.

A good marriage must be predicated upon the Scriptures and operate under the influence of the Spirit of God. Any person who wants to hold an office in the church must prove himself, and his sanction is based on the order in his home. This is how highly God esteems marriage: He bases our other opportunities to serve Him on how well we handle marriage. Satan knows this and he also knows that if he can destroy the home, he can destroy the church. Many people confess that "Jesus is Lord," speaking in a heavenly language, but they go right back outside and raise hell. It doesn't take much to live right during the short span of time in which you are in the church building. You can deceive the pastor, but you can't deceive God. There's nothing that takes place that God does not have knowledge of: "The eyes of the Lord are in every place, beholding the evil and the good" (Proverbs 15:3).

I love the principle of sowing and reaping, or seedtime and harvest, but I am aware that most people have only limited understanding of how this principle works. Most people are only familiar with the positive aspects of sowing and reaping. For example, if you sow love and mercy, you will reap love and mercy. And if you sow goodness and kindness, you will reap the same. We all love this; it sounds so nice. If you want good, you do good. Great. But what about the other side of the coin.

Reaping the Whirlwind

> *Therefore all things whatsoever ye would that men should do to you, do ye even so to them....*

Matthew 7:12

> *For they have sown the wind, and they shall reap the whirlwind: it hath no stalk: the bud shall yield no meal: if so be it yield, the strangers shall swallow it up.*

Hosea 8:7

We cannot negate the fact that the principle of seedtime and harvest works whether you sow good or bad seed: you will reap whatever you sow. As we said earlier, if you sow love, you'll reap love; if it's joy, then you'll receive joy. But on the other hand, if what you sow is negative, then what you reap will be the same. Have you ever heard the expression "sow the wind and reap the whirlwind?" It means "to engage in, and suffer the consequences of, evil or folly" (Hosea 8:7). This is the negative side to the sowing and reaping principle. And don't forget the principle of multiplication--you will always reap more than you sow. When you walk in the Spirit, you reap eternal life and peace. That's a greater return! But when you sow to the flesh, you reap death. That's a greater return, too! But it's a greater return on the negative side. Who in their right mind wants that! According to John 3:6, ''That which is born of the flesh is flesh; and that which is born of the Spirit is spirit.'' It is a kingdom principle which states that if you sow to the flesh, you will reap corruption, while sowing to the spirit will cause you to reap eternal life. The principles of God do not stop operating just because we choose to move on the negative side.

There are some people who still have not grasped the positive side of sowing and reaping. Because of the circumstances of their lives, they feel they've only sowed and never reaped. The devil has deceived them into thinking that their efforts have been in vain, and he has caused them to think that their positive sowing has actually yielded a negative reward. Nothing could be further from the truth! The devil has always sought to pervert godly principles; he has always attempted to deceive the people of God. Satan likes nothing better than for the people of God to accuse God, saying He's failed to uphold His word. We must wake up and realize that God cannot fail to uphold His word. God intends for us to be used. If we're never used, we never grow. It's part of the process. We don't need to worry about the motives of others. You'll never be able to figure them out anyway, and you'll drive yourself crazy trying. All God requires is that we be led by His Spirit, and sow when we should. If we sow into the lives of those whose motives are impure, that's not our problem. God will take care of the matter, and He will use those seemingly negative experiences to produce some positive results in our lives. The reason He can do that is because whenever you sow something positive, even if the recipient is moving in deception or with ungodly motive, God will give you a positive reward.

The Reproduction Process

> *And God said, Let the earth bring forth grass, the herb yielding seed, and the fruit tree yielding fruit after his kind, whose seed is in itself, upon the earth: and it was so.*
>
> *And the earth brought forth grass, and herb yielding seed after his kind, and the tree yielding fruit, whose seed was in itself, after his kind: and God saw that it was good.*

Genesis 1:11-12

God instituted the principle of sowing and reaping, or seedtime and harvest. This principle is that everything reproduces after its own kind. Let's look at how God implemented this process.

> *And God said, Let the waters bring forth abundantly the moving creature that hath life, and fowl that may fly above the earth in the open firmament of heaven.*
>
> *And God created great whales, and every living creature that moveth, which the waters brought forth abundantly, after their kind, and every winged fowl after his kind: and God saw that it was good.*
>
> *And God blessed them, saying, Be fruitful, and multiply, and fill the waters in the seas, and let fowl multiply in the earth.*

And the evening and the morning were the fifth day.

Genesis 1:20-23

God created great, winged beings to fly in the firmament (sky). He filled the waters (seas) with creatures whose habitation is in the water. He gave them the same principle of the grass and the fruit trees--to reproduce after their own kind.

And God said, Let us make man in our image, after our likeness: and let them have dominion over the fish of the sea, and over the fowl of the air, and over the cattle, and over all the earth, and over every creeping thing that creepeth upon the earth.

So God created man in his own image, in the image of God created he him; male and female created he them.

And God blessed them, and God said unto them, Be fruitful, and multiply, and replenish the earth, and subdue it: and have dominion over the fish of the sea, and over the fowl of the air, and over every living thing that moveth upon the earth.

Genesis 1:26-28

When God created man and woman, they were to be fruitful, multiply and replenish (repopulate) the earth. This was the same principle given to the vegetable and animal kingdoms. Everything is to reproduce after its own kind. If you don't get anything else out of this book, get this verse of Scripture:

*While the earth remaineth, seedtime and harvest,
and cold and heat, and summer and winter, and
day and night shall not cease.*

Genesis 8:22

The principle of seedtime and harvest and seasonal change, shall never cease while the earth remains. God is saying that unless the seed is planted, there can be no harvest; and as long as the earth remains, seasonal change will come. But to receive the harvest, man must initiate the planting of the seed, and he must plant according to the return that he desires.

If the average farmer knew what the average saint knows about seedtime and harvest then there would be no food in the grocery stores. What this should say to you is that believers are living way below their privilege when it comes to spiritual matters. The farmer doesn't sit on his porch all day, sipping a drink and relaxing. He works! And he works hard. Why? Because he understands that if he doesn't work, if he doesn't plant and then tend that which he has planted, he won't have a crop. He understands that after he has planted, the soil must be watered and nurtured in order to produce a crop. Why do we, as believers, let this principle pass us by? Why do we view ourselves as a people exempt from this law? We need to wake up and understand that until we do what the Bible says to do, the way the Bible says to do it, we will not reap what we desire. Although it is God who gives the increase (1 Corinthians 3:6), we are responsible for the planting and watering.

Sowing the Word

The sower soweth the word.

Mark 4:14

Simple, but profound. Jesus has made it very clear that you don't need anyone else to sow the word in you; you can read it for yourself. When you accept this responsibility, you will do something about it. You won't be one of those people whose works are going to burn up when they stand before the Lord. So many people want to blame the pastor for what they don't know. But God knows you have Bibles; God knows you have access to His word. And God knows if you've sought after His word, or if you've been content to be fed a malnourished diet, complaining all the time that you didn't like it. If you know your spiritual diet is bad, God is expecting you to do something about it. Now! You're not going to be able to convince God that "the devil made you do it" (Like Flip Wilson used to say). You won't be able to justify your actions before God. He won't accept any of your excuses. Look at the case of Adam and Eve:

> *And he said, Who told thee that thou wast naked? Hast thou eaten of the tree, whereof I commanded thee that thou shouldest not eat?*
>
> *And the man said, The woman whom thou gavest to be with me, she gave me of the tree, and I did eat.*
>
> *And the Lord God said unto the woman, What is this that thou hast done? And the woman said, The serpent beguiled me, and I did eat.*

Genesis 3:11-13

Who were they trying to kid? God didn't go for it then, and He's not going for it now. God accepts no excuses because He knows the truth! He knows what He gave us. He knows we have opportunities to study His word, to sow it into our lives.

He knows we have access to it. If when we stand before God in judgment, we try to get Him to buy our feeble excuses, we will be faced with a rude awakening. We need to start being honest with ourselves and begin to plant God's word in our lives now so that His will might come to pass in our lives.

God dealt respectively with the serpent, Adam, and Eve regarding their sins. Not one of them bore the sins of the other. They all stood alone. And although the man is the leader of his home, he is not the sin bearer. We are all responsible for our own actions. That's the way God set it up. But he wants us to remember that He is a God of love. That's why He created the human family--to express His love through us. But then man sinned, and they began to produce a fallen race.

A Fallen Image

> *And Adam lived an hundred and thirty years, and begat a son in his own likeness, after his image; and called his name Seth.*

> Genesis 5:3

Seth was born after the image and likeness of Adam in his fallen state. A fallen image. God gave Adam the command to be fruitful, multiply, and replenish the earth before the fall, not after it. Being made in the image and likeness of God, they were going to reproduce after their perfect state. But then sin entered the picture. And because of sin, Adam and Eve reproduced a fallen image of what God had originally created. It was an image that now bore the curse of sin. As a result of this sin curse, mankind would only be able to reproduce the kind that it had now become--a fallen race of people with a sinful nature.

If a person has not received Jesus, he is under the curse. Even when an individual is born-again, he still has the thoughts of the curse. That knowledge has to be torn down and replaced with the pure, unadulterated, uncompromising word of the Lord. Then they will have within them the seed that will produce the image that God wants. From the beginning, God's mode of operation was to speak things into existence. He sowed His word and it produced for Him. We are to do the same.

Sowing in Season

> *To every thing there is a season, and a time to every purpose under the heaven.*

Ecclesiastes 3:1

When you sow has a lot to do with what you will reap. If you are attempting to sow into the life of your marriage partner, but your timing is wrong, you will not achieve the results you'd hoped for. So many marriages are unsuccessful because the marriage partners did not understand this principle. And pertaining to the wives, who have so much to do with the application of this principle, this is where the ministry of the godly woman must come in. Sadly, this has been lacking in the church. We don't have enough mature women teaching the younger women how to love their husbands and run their households.

Most singles have not been taught how and when to sow, either. And once again, the importance of the woman's ministry is revealed. In the courting situation, women need to understand when to plant and what to plant into the lives of their future mates. When a woman takes a seed and throws it at a man whose "ground" has not first been broken up, he will be unable to respond, and she will not see the desired results. This can be frustrating for women. So even before they marry, it is helpful for women to learn this principle about breaking up the ground.

The farmer doesn't go out and try to sow when he knows that the ground is hard and frozen; he knows it must first be broken up--made receptive to the seed. And sometimes he recognizes that it's just not time to sow. It's the same way in the marital relationship--sometimes it's not time to sow. My entire ministry is based on the principle of sowing and reaping, because of what the Bible says about it: "While the earth remaineth, seedtime and harvest, and cold and heat, and summer and winter, and day and night shall not cease" (Genesis 8:22). Yet, I still know that there is a season within which to sow.

You must sow in season, when the Holy Spirit leads you. Because so many Christian women have mishandled this, many of their unsaved husbands perceive them as preachers. God did not call you to be a preacher to your husband, because you'll never win him by preaching to him; you're to share with him. You're to share with him from the position of being his wife, and not just from being a woman. As a wife you can do some things that you could not do as just a woman. Take for example a wife who's looking through a salespaper and sees that there is a sale on an item she really wants. She begins to think about it and decides how she would like to handle the situation. As a wife, she has a couple of options. One works, one doesn't. Let's look at both of them.

In a situation like this, many women would meet their husbands at the door when they return home from work, and without hardly a greeting they'd say, "There's something on sale that I want. It's 5:00 p.m. and the store closes at 5:30 p.m.

Hurry! We've got to make it before the store closes.'' What do
you think his response will be? In most cases, it would be
negative. And even if she did manage to drag him there, it
would be against his will. Wouldn't you rather have a willing
husband to join you in the things you want to do? Of course
you would. So let's look at the second option. And remember,
we'll be dealing with the principle of breaking up the ground.

   The same thing happens. You have a sale you want to
go to. The first thing you do different is recognize that if the
time of the sale is such that you can't make it, you just can't
make it. So you commit the matter into the hands of the Lord
and move on. But let's just suppose that this particular sale
extends into the next day. This is perfect because it gives you
time to minister (notice I said minister--God called wives to
minister to their husbands) to your husband and prepare him
for your request. In other words, you can break up the ground
before you plant the seed. (Now keep in mind that you are
 operating as a godly woman and so your request will probably
be in order anyway. But if it is unreasonable and your husband
has to deny you, you must still remain in your position as a
submissive wife. Even if it's reasonable and he denies you for
some reason, that's when you turn the matter over to God, you
don't fight, and He will work it out for you). So by the time
he arrives home, you've already prepared his dinner. When he
walks in, after you greet him with a kiss, he smells the
delicious aroma of roast beef (wives, are you getting the
picture?). Then he walks into the dining room and finds the
table set with candles and your best table setting. He notices
there are only two plates. ''Where are the children?'', he asks.
You respond by saying, ''The children are at their grandparents' house.'' So it's just the two of you.

   After you minister the meal to him, and he's feeling
good, cared for, refreshed, you say to him ''Honey, let's sit on

the love seat....'' Later, while the two of you are relaxing, enjoying one another's company, you say, ''Honey, there's an item downtown that I'd like to have.'' Now wives, you tell me, what do you think he'll say? That's right. ''Anything you want, darling'' will probably be the response. Why? Because in your ministry to him you converted him. You broke up his ground before you planted your seed, so your seed was received and it brought forth that which you desired. You have to use some wisdom when planting.

The principles of sowing and reaping include this: before you can sow the seed, it is imperative that you cultivate the ground. Once the seed it sown, then you water it with your confession, which is the word of God. After this takes place, then you can begin to reap the harvest.

Success in Marriage

The success of your marriage is based on your obedience to the word of God. The success of the church in these last days hinges on our homes--not on some crusade or revival service. Wives, in order for you to have a successful marriage, you must first have a repentant heart. But even before repentance, there must be forgiveness and an acknowledgement that you have done some things wrong. This is the foundation for a successful marriage.

Wives, let your husbands function in their God-given roles. Pray for him, esteem him highly, and encourage him. Help him to become everything God wants him to be. By releasing him to God, you'll release yourself, and this will pave the way for success in your marriage. And don't allow the devil to cause you to think that you must carry the household burdens. God never intended for wives to bear that burden. He never intended for wives to have to worry about finances, or how the mortgage, food and clothing bills would be paid. Some of you are no doubt asking, ''But what if God doesn't do it?'' Don't worry--God won't fail you! Just trust Him. You never know how your husband will respond to the move of God in his life. Let him know that you are praying for him, and that you want him to run your home. Then step back and watch him become all that God wants him to be.

Expectation

> *Give, and it shall be given unto you; good measure, pressed down, and shaken together, and running over, shall men give into your bosom. For with the same measure that ye mete withal it shall be measured to you again.*

> Luke 6:38

If you don't give, don't expect anything! If you don't plant, don't expect a harvest!

> *Therefore the heaven over you is stayed from dew, and the earth is stayed from her fruit.*

> *And I called for a drought upon the land, and upon the mountains, and upon the corn, and upon the new wine, and upon the oil, and upon that which the ground bringeth forth, and upon men, and upon cattle, and upon all the labour of the hands.*

> Haggai 1:10-11

Wives, even as you read about the virtuous woman in

Proverbs 31, You must realize that while she is the apex or zenith of womanhood, she had to go through a process to get there. And a process is just that--something that occurs over a period of time, having its up and down moments. It's not always easy. And because it doesn't just happen without your effort, the first thing you need to do is begin to plant the seeds that will cause you to be like her. You may have to go to your husband and say, "I'm sorry, but I love you and I haven't been the wife that I should be. I haven't given you the support that you've needed. I haven't esteemed and honored you. But from this moment forth everything that God wants of me, I will produce." This is how you begin to sow seeds that will bring forth good fruit in its season.

God is quick when it comes to confirming His word. When the word of the Lord goes forth, He immediately wants to confirm it. That means that you should walk in expectation. You should live as though at any moment you expect God to do something and move on your behalf. I'm telling you to get greedy whenever the word of God comes to you. The more desire you have for His word, the more this spirit of expectation will arise in you.

I always pray, "Lord, feed my soul with the substance of thyself that I come short in nothing." You want God to feed you until you want nothing else. Every word of God is energized with the very life and nature of God. The reason we have so many dead churches is because people don't eat the word. They become distracted by what is going on instead of who they supposedly came to worship.

Worship is a time of great expectation. God expects us to worship Him, and we in turn should be in expectation to receive from Him, for the Bible says, "But thou art holy, O thou that inhabitest the praises of Israel [your people]" (Psalm 22:3). The presence of God ANYWHERE is cause for expectation! So church is not the time for you to be concerned about what clothing someone has on, or the cold and indifferent person who may be sitting next to you. Let those type of people know that you are there in expectation. You're drawing waters out of ''the wells of salvation'' (Isaiah 12:3). Let them know that the joy of the Lord is your strength. Show them by your worship that you know that in the presence of God there is fullness of joy (Psalms 16:11). When you stand in expectation like that, you will have an affect on those around you.

In studying how to have the God-kind of marriage, it is our goal that you succeed in everything that you do, and that you reach the conclusion that God desires for you to have His best. God has given us His blueprint for success--the Bible. It is God's desire that every person become successful, whether married, single, widowed, or divorced. You cannot undo the mistakes of yesterday, but you can have hope and plant seeds of success for today. Whatever you are experiencing this day is a result of what you planted into your life some time ago. But even if it's negative, you can change it. The Bible says, ''If ye be willing and obedient, ye shall eat the good of the land'' (Isaiah 1:19). Line up with God's word and stand in expectation for the wonderful things that are coming your way!

God's will is for you to have His best! Having God's best does not necessarily mean that He is going to make you a millionaire (but He might). Nor does it necessarily mean that you're going to become the president of a corporation (but you will if it's His will for you). Having God's best means that you use whatever He has given you for His glory. Whatever talents, skills, and abilities you may possess, God wants them to function to the maximum according to His word and by His Spirit. This is having God's best. Everyone of us should be success-minded, not failure-prone. Believers don't have time for failure. We should not be succumbing, but overcoming. We should not be just getting along, but reigning.

I want you to remember that there is a time to plant, and a time to reap; and God is in charge of the season. While you can't do anything to rush the season, you can nurture the seed that you've planted. Water and feed it. Watch over it. As a result of the curse of the law that dominates the earth, that which is opposite of God comes automatically. For example, when you plant tomato seeds, you cultivate the ground, choosing the proper location, then planting and watering. After a few days, even with the proper care, you begin to notice little weeds. If you allow them to remain, they will choke the life out of the tomato seeds. It is the same way with your life.

The negative will come, even when you plant spiritual seeds (I should say especially when you plant spiritual seeds!). This is why it is so necessary for you to stand on your confession of faith. A lot of wives will say, ''I've been praying and praying for my husband, but he hasn't changed yet. In fact, he's gotten worse!'' Don't worry, it doesn't mean a thing. Just keep standing on God's word. You may find that once you start to labor on your husband's behalf, fasting and doing spiritual warfare, that his behavior will worsen. Don't be intimidated by this tactic of Satan! Remember that the devil comes immediately in an attempt to choke the word. But he is stupid, and if you stay fastened onto the things of God you will see right through what he is doing. His attempts won't sway you at all. Remember the word of the Lord: ''And let us not be weary in well doing: for in due season we shall reap, if we faint not'' (Galatians 6:9). Don't give up!

Whether you know it or not, while you are on this earth you are sowing something every day. This is why I admonish wives to quit degrading their unsaved husbands by putting

them down with their words. Don't see them as unsaved. You
need to put into operation the principle of speaking those
things that be not as though they were. Get excited about what
God can do and stand in expectation. See your husband as a
Spirit-filled man, speaking in tongues, under your pastor's
wings, and on fire for God. See him as a mighty man of valor,
excelling in spiritual things. Look at him through God's eyes,
and begin to see him as a man made in the image and likeness
of God Himself. This is walking in expectation. It takes faith,
and God will help you, because it's pleasing to Him.

Receive the Increase

> *And let us not be weary in well doing: for in due
> season we shall reap, if we faint not.*

Galatians 6:9

> *To every thing there is a season, and a time to
> every purpose under the heaven.*

Ecclesiastes 3:1

Don't get weary in well doing. God intends for you to
keep planting. Paul said to Titus, ''The aged women likewise,
that they be in behavior as becometh holiness, not false
accuser, not given to much wine, teachers of good things [not
bad things]'' (Titus 2:3). Good things. We have to continue in
good things.

I remember the time there was an incident in our
church in which a couple's marriage was breaking down
which resulted in their wanting to separate. Some of the
women in our fellowship rose to the support of the wife by
providing a haven and money, which enabled her to leave her

husband. Because of the circumstances surrounding the separation, it was sin for these other sisters to be involved in this situation. I confronted them and commanded them to repent, and not be involved in this matter any longer. Where marital problems are concerned, the best approach for anyone on the outside to take is to not get involved. For the most part, God can better work things out without your help. The best thing you could possible do is to stay on your face in prayer and leave the matter in the hands of God. We must remember that the marital relationship is a very intimate association. There are things that won't be shared with you, even though one of the parties may be your best friend. That is why it is best to leave it in the hands of God. He knows all the details and you can rest assured that He will work it out to the very best possible solution.

I can remember back to the time when one of my daughters wanted to leave her husband because of a little ''run-in'' they had one day. She called me, told me she was leaving, and asked me if she could come to my house. (She asked if she could come, but I could tell from the response that followed that she actually expected me to say yes.) But I told her ''No.'' She couldn't believe I was refusing her request and said, ''What do you mean?'' So I explained it: ''Just what I said--you can't come!'' I still have two other daughters at home, and they will never know that a wife can leave her husband and come home to her father in this house, because when they leave they're not coming back either.'' I sound like a real bad guy, don't I? But I really had no choice. If her situation had been different, if her well-being had been threatened, if she was in danger, I would have responded differently. But that was not the case. Young women in the church must learn that marriage is a commitment--on the good days and on the bad.

Well, I guess I don't need to tell you what her response was. She slammed down the phone and didn't speak to me for a year. That hurt me, but I knew I had told her the truth. And I also knew that she was not rebelling against me, but against the truth. And God has a way of working things out (even for strong-willed people like me and my children!).

She finally came around. God got a hold to her, and she gave her life back to Him. But she was still at her own home. See, you don't have to compromise biblical principles in your efforts to have things turn out right. In fact, if you do compromise them, things won't turn out the way you want them to anyway. No one has the right to tell anyone else that they should leave their spouse. If they leave, let it be on their own--then it's between them and God, just the way it should be.

Parents who let their children come back home every time they have a little fight with their spouse are making a grave mistake (they're really helping to kill their child's marriage). When you do this, you're sowing seeds of discord. In these situations, there are always two families involved-- the husband's and wife's. When the woman gets mad and runs home where her parents receive her, how do you think the other family feels? It is only obvious that they are going to side with their son. Discord. Avoid it.

In the case of domestic problems, people tend to identify with flesh and blood: "This is my daughter; she has to be right...This is my son; he's right." It doesn't matter that the son may have hit the daughter; he's still right, according to his family. And even if the daughter refuses to care for her home the way she knows she should, in her family's eyes, she is still right. Utter nonsense! There is no place in the kingdom of God for such carrying on. Situations like this can at times get so messy that the son or daughter-in-law is actually forbidden to enter the in-laws home any longer. God has a better way.

You must understand that the spirit of righteousness, or of a willingness to do genuine good, is operated by God. The influence of evil is operated by the devil, through the curse. God will see to it that whatever you do in love will come back to you. Whatever you plant, God will see to it that you get it back in its season. He's the Lord of the harvest. If you sow to the Spirit, God will see to it that the Spirit brings you the manifestation of that which you have sown:

> *I have planted, Apollos watered; but God gave the increase.*

> 1 Corinthians 3:6

You do not have control over the time of the season. However, you do have control over the planting and watering of the seed. Remember, you shall reap, if you do not give up.

Chapter Thirteen

Faith

Now faith is the substance of things hoped for, the evidence of things not seen.

For by it the elders obtained a good report.

Through faith we understand that the worlds were framed by the word of God, so that things which are seen were not made of things which do appear.

By faith Abel offered unto God a more excellent sacrifice than Cain, by which he obtained witness that he was righteous, God testifying of his gifts: and by it he being dead yet speaketh.

By faith Enoch was translated that he should not see death; and was not found, because God had translated him: for before his translation he had this testimony, that he pleased God.

But without faith it is impossible to please him: for he that cometh to God must believe that he is, and that he is a rewarder of them that diligently seek him.

Hebrews 11:1-6

If you are going to have the God-kind of marriage, you must use your faith. God cannot move in your direction without faith. It is impossible to please God without faith.

 You must come to God realizing that whatever He said He is, He is. God, the omnipotent, omniscient one, expressed Himself through the human family, making man and woman in His image and after His likeness. Then He instructed them to multiply and replenish the earth, reproducing the God-kind of seed. Had Adam and Eve obeyed the word of God, the earth today would be filled with the image and likeness of God, expressed through the human family. Instead, through sin, the earth has been filled with a fallen image of God's creation. Instead of the original perfection that God had created, there is corruption. So many marriages are operating from this corrupted condition. Many people feel there is no hope for their marriage. But there is always hope. When Jesus came to redeem mankind from their sinful state, one of the things He purchased with His life and blood was our marriages. So you must have faith that God is able to restore your marriage to the God-kind of marriage. But in order for faith to work in your marriage, you must hold on to your hope.

 Faith is not futuristic. The Bible says that faith "is." Faith is present--it's not futuristic and it's not past. But it is the substance of things hoped for. In other words, your faith is proof that you're hoping for something. And because you are hoping for something, your actions reflect that. Which leads us right into the Scripture found in James on works: "For as the body without the spirit is dead, so faith without works is dead also" (James 2:26). Your faith will cause the things you hope for to be manifested in your life. And the manifestation or realization of these things becomes the proof of what you've hoped for. Are you getting this? You can't look at your marriage and say it won't work when God has already gone on record as saying, "Is there anything too hard for the Lord?" (Genesis 18:14). We need to start taking God at His word.

Consider this illustration of how faith works so you can apply it to your marriage. An archaeologist went to Asia in search of a discovery. He dug and dug until he found a bone. Encouraged by his finding, he continued to dig until he eventually uncovered a whole dinosaur. Quite excited by his discovery, he said, ''These bones represent a great dinosaur that lived in another era!'' It was the biggest discovery that anyone had ever made. He and his assistants were so excited that they began to dance about, rejoicing. They were so happy, because now they had proof that the great creature actually existed! Then all of a sudden, they heard a loud noise coming over the hill. They turned around, looked up, and to their utter amazement, there stood a great, big dinosaur--in living color! At that moment, they were no longer operating in belief only. At that moment, they actually knew. Right before them stood the proof of their belief.

Since the same principle applies in the spirit realm, what is the proof of your belief? If you have a financial need, you believe God for your finances. If you're in need of healing, then you stand on His word for your healing. What are we saying? Faith changes things. If you want something from God, learn what His word says and stand on it. God declares faith to be current, now. In the same way that you believe God for finances or healing, you can believe God for a good marriage. God wants to meet your every need--spirit, soul, and body. He will do it. Just walk in the God-kind of faith.

Diligent Seekers

But without faith it is impossible to please him: for he that cometh to God must believe that he is, and that he is a rewarder of them that diligently seek him.

Hebrews 11:6

If you have a broken marriage, God desires to heal it. And He will move on your behalf, based upon how much you seek Him. To be a diligent seeker means that with a steady, painstaking effort, you are busily seeking God for a solution to your problem. THE EFFORT MUST COME FROM YOU. God wants to help you, but you must present yourself to Him in order for Him to move on your behalf.

If you want a good marriage, you must do everything within your power to be a good mate. Paul expresses this so clearly in the book of Ephesians, yet we often take it out of context: ''...and having done all ... stand'' (Ephesians 6:13). As believers, we often focus on the ''standing'' part, but forget about the ''having done all'' part. We must understand that if we don't do it all, we won't be able to stand. If we say we want a good marriage, but we fail to make the effort, we will not have a good marriage. It is just not possible. Anywhere we give the devil place, he will come in and attempt to destroy. 1 Peter 5:8 says, ''Be sober, be vigilant; because your adversary the devil, as a roaring lion, walketh about, seeking whom he may devour.'' Satan has plans for your marriage--destruction! He is doing everything within his power to see that your marriage doesn't work. But he doesn't have a chance of succeeding if you become a diligent pursuer of God.

In order for you to pursue God in this way you must lose your misconceptions about Him. I don't care how many preachers say it, God is not the source of your problem, and He's not trying to teach you something through some problem that He's created for you. Man was created in the image and likeness of God. Man was given dominion so that whatever he permits can tie-up the hand of God. In other words, because man is a free will moral agent, with the ability to choose his own course, God allows him to do so. Most of the problems in our lives are there as a result of a wrong choice that we have made. Whether we made it based on misinformation or just because we didn't care enough to do any better, we are still the responsible party, not God. And then after we've done our part, that is when the door is open for the devil, and he gladly walks in to do whatever he can to make things worse. That is how it works. And we need to get it straight now. We have the choice. And our choice will determine the outcome.

> *But of the tree of the knowledge of good and evil,*
> *thou shalt not eat of it: for in the day that thou*
> *eatest thereof thou shalt surely die.*

Genesis 2:17

Adam was exercising his free will when he ate the fruit. The result of his action was death--for himself and all mankind. God is not the cause of the sickness, misery, and pain that is so prevalent in our world today. Yet, the devil has always tried to influence people to believe that God is the source of their problems. God's not the source--He's the solution!

God doesn't put cancer on people. He doesn't give them heart trouble or any other illness or disease you can think of. God doesn't cause you to lose your job, or inflict injury on your children. God never attempts to destroy our marriages. Yet this is the image that some people (believers!) have of God. I could never understand how people suffering with an illness could believe that God would put it on them. At the same time that they call for the preacher, they're saying that it is God's will for them to suffer. If you are suffering for the will of God, and you know it's the will of God, why call the elder to pray for you? If this sounds like it doesn't make sense, that is because it doesn't.

Adam and Eve were in a perfect environment. Then the

devil came. God didn't intervene when Satan began to seduce Eve (but you do know that He knew what was going on), because He had already given His word (command) to Adam, His representative. Adam was there, and God knew that he knew what to do. (God's way is really quite simple if we stop to think about it.) God had already told Adam that he had dominion over everything that crept upon the face of the earth. All they had to do was resist Satan; he would have had no choice but to flee (James 4:7). But they chose another course (notice I said "they chose." God didn't do it!) Adam simply failed to exercise his God-given dominion.

The problem with the church today is we do not believe God gave us dominion. Have you ever encountered people who know nothing about God debating the things of God? If it wasn't so sad, it might be amusing. And this is how so many in the church are. Quick to debate, but hardly know a thing about God. They haven't opened their Bibles to find out what He says, yet they think they are experts on His word. And sometimes even the people who read their Bibles don't really understand what God is saying.

I'm reminded of a mother of three who after being married for only three years, lost her husband. At the funeral, the minister said, "The Lord has given, and the Lord has taken away; Blessed be the name of the Lord." Now while I agree with the "Blessed be the name of the Lord" part, I believe he took the other portion of Scripture out of its context. Why would God give this woman a husband and children, and then take the husband away? It doesn't make any sense. And even more importantly, it doesn't line up with what the scriptures reveal to us about God. In speaking of the devil, the Bible says, "The thief cometh not, but for to steal, and to kill, and to destroy: I am come that they might have life, and that they might have it more abundantly" (John 10:10). Satan steals;

Satan kills; Satan destroys. Not God. He is the great enabler
who will enable you to make it. He is the life-giver who will
sustain you in the midst of all your trials. He is not only able,
as most churches will tell you, but He is able and willing to do
''exceedingly abundantly above all that we ask or think''
(Ephesians 3:20). Just become a diligent seeker of Him.

Too Hard?

> *Is anything too hard for the Lord?*
>
> Genesis 18:14

    I'd like to present a little scenario to the wives.
Suppose you met your spouse while traveling on an airplane.
He professed Christianity, said all the right things, and you
fell for it. Then after marrying him, the truth surfaces. Now
you are faced with the reality of your situation. What should
you do? Even though this man may not have been the one God
meant for you to marry, what's done is done. Now you need
to think about what God can do for your marriage. If you
understand that it is God's will for you to experience the God-
kind of marriage, the ideal marriage, then you can bypass the
circumstances and put pressure on His word.

    God has given us a blueprint for a successful marriage.
We are without excuses. You may or may not feel you need a
marriage counselor, but one thing you do need is to make the
quality decision to submit to the word of God. Submitting to
the word of God releases the life and nature of God, which is
incorporated within His word. God's nature is literally released into your situation when you become a doer of the
word.

    You were reproduced after humankind; everyone has

a mother and a father. The union from which you were produced caused you to be raised in a certain environment. This environment shaped you into who you would become. It had an effect on your emotions, your intellect, and even your financial stability. Most people are the product of two to three godless generations, thus they do not know what God has to say concerning them.

The marriage that you saw the most of was based on the home you lived in--whether it was your natural parents, step-parents, grandparents, foster parents, or even an aunt and uncle. What you have been exposed to has a bearing on your present way of thinking and living. Many people have an inability for growth because they will not exercise their will to change their own situations.

Yet, you can actually take God's word and change your life. However, you must first admit that you were wrong about some things. The Bible teaches emphatically that everything reproduces after its own kind. We can see this reproductive law in operation at every level of life--vegetable, animal and human.

While visiting with friends in Atlanta, Georgia, they took my wife and I to see the Martin Luther King Center for Social Non-Violence. Dr. King's family history is amazing. The Ebenezer Baptist Church was founded by his grandfather, Reverend Williams. A proud man, he was blessed with a keen intellect and tremendous ability. He led the first boycott in Georgia, and established the first black high school there as well. His son-in-law, who pastored the Ebenezer Baptist Church after Martin Luther King Jr.'s father held the position, led the first boycott of a newspaper in Georgia.

Dr. King's way of thinking did not come from out of nowhere--he was the product of his environment. At a time when such living conditions were not common for black people, Rev. Williams had a twelve room home with heat and running water; it is still standing today. He was a prominent man with a healthy mentality. He thought well of himself and the God that was in him. He would not allow anyone to take this away from him.

Understand this--the devil can't take anything away from you except he uses another person to do it. Sometimes the devil will try to get to you through your mate or your children; that is when you have to know who you are in God. The issue is not who you are, but who you are in God. It doesn't matter what your gender is, your race, culture or your social standing. What matters is are you a believer? Are you a son or daughter of God?

The Abundant Life

> *...I am come that they might have life, and that they might have it more abundantly.*

John 10:10

The abundant life that Jesus is referring to in this Scripture is to be lived right here and now. It is not something that is reserved for heaven. Heaven will take care of itself. There is a life that God wants us to live on this earth, that will testify to who He is. It is the abundant life. If the principles of God don't work down here, how do we know they will work in heaven? God wants us to prove Him here. Now.

Some people are so "spiritual" (I use the term with reservation) that they fail to remember they are still living a life that is based on this earth. They walk around with their heads up in the air, carrying a big Bible under their arms, yet failing to realize what God is really requiring of us. Their response for everything is, ''The Lord understands....'' Yes, God does understand. But along with that He's given us guidelines on how to conduct our lives, and if we follow them our lives will take a decidedly positive turn. Yes, He understands, but that doesn't mean He wants you to stay in the place where you're at. He expects you to look into His word, find out what you can do to change your situation, and do it. When you fail to do this, in God's eyes, you are moving in ignorance. Reading God's word will not only make you aware of His will for you, but it will eliminate all your excuses for staying where you are. There are lying spirits in the earth. Their purpose is to deceive you and keep you from learning the truth about God's will for you. The Bible says, ''Beloved, believe not every spirit, but try the spirits whether they are of God...'' (1 John 4:1). A knowledge of God's word will enable you to recognize those spirits that are not of God.

The abundant life is a principle that God intended to be expressed in marriages. God did not intend for you to get married and allow the devil to tear your house apart. God wants you to take His word and apply it to your lives. His word, which is charged with His nature and life, will release the abundant life into your marriage, and give you power to keep the devil in his place--under your feet!

God's ideal for marriage is that you reach your maximized potential and experience the zenith or utopia in your marriage relationship. There is a dimension of marriage and household relationships that you have never imagined you could enter into. God has designed the marital relationship to be a type of His relationship to the church--Christ the groom, the church as His bride. It is the highest possible relationship that man can enter into apart from his relationship with God. And even though we're just scratching the surface, we're on our way to realizing the God-kind of marriages. By staying full of the Holy Ghost, and walking in line with the word of God, we are sure to get there. We can make it if we keep His word.

I'd like to leave you with the words of our Lord Jesus Christ, as recorded in the book of John, chapter 14, verse 21:

> *He that hath my commandments, and keepeth them, he it is that loveth me: and he that loveth me shall be loved of my Father, and I will love him, and will manifest myself to him.*

GOD BLESS YOU.

Notes

Notes

Notes

Notes

Notes

Notes

Notes

Notes

Other Books By Andrew Merritt

Pursue, Overtake and Reclaim
Jesus Destroyed the Works of the Devil

For Further Information or Tapes write:

Straight Gate Church
10100 Grand River Ave.
Detroit, MI 48204-0389